'An excellent user-friendly set of principles in order to help the Bible reader understand and apply its message with increasing confidence and relevance.'
David Jackman, President, The Proclamation Trust

'This book is a first-class tool kit to help in the reading and understanding of the Bible. The Bible is a book for every Christian to read and hear the voice of God. It is not just the domain of the Christian scholar. A person does not have to be an intellectual to read and understand the Bible. In fact obedience to what is clear is often the key to understanding what is at first reading unclear. My prayer is that this tool kit will encourage more and more Christians to approach the Bible with renewed vigour.'
John Chapman, Australian evangelist

'Nigel and Andrew have written a great work on knowing God better, learning his will for your life and reading your Bible. I like it. In fact, I think we'll start using it at our church.'
Mark Dever, Pastor, Capitol Hill Baptist Church, Washington DC, and Director, 9marks.org

About the authors

Nigel: I'm married to Elisa and we have two children, Jacob and Greta. Having become a Christian while at school, I was active in the Christian Union at Durham University and then tried out Christian work in a church for a year. After a brief stint in industry I trained to be a vicar at theological college, and then worked as a curate for three years at St Matthew's, Fulham. For the last seven years I've been the student minister at St Helen's, Bishopsgate, in London, where I met and worked with Andrew. I enjoy rugby and taking Elisa out to nice restaurants.

Andrew: I became a Christian during my first year of university. I enjoyed student life so much that I've managed to spin it out for almost nine years now. I went on to do a PhD in human hearing in York and am now studying for a theological degree at Oak Hill College in preparation for ordained ministry. In between, I spent three years working under Nigel, teaching the gospel to students in London. I enjoy spending time with my godson (to whom this book is partly dedicated), playing Bach badly on the piano, hunting for bargains in second-hand bookshops and watching *The West Wing*.

DIG DEEPER!

Tools to unearth the Bible's treasure

Nigel Beynon and Andrew Sach

ivp

INTER-VARSITY PRESS
38 De Montfort Street, Leicester LE1 7GP, England
Email: ivp@ivp-editorial.co.uk
Website: www.ivpbooks.com

First published 2005

British Library Cataloguing-in-Publication Data
A catalogue record for this book is available from the British Library.

ISBN-13: 978-1-84474-103-8
ISBN-10: 1-84474-103-6

Set in Dante 10.5/13 pt
Typeset in Great Britain by CRB Associates, Reepham, Norfolk
Printed and bound in Great Britain by Ashford Colour Press Ltd,
Gosport, Hampshire

Inter-Varsity Press is the publishing division of the Universities and Colleges
Christian Fellowship (formerly the Inter-Varsity Fellowship), a student movement
linking Christian Unions in universities and colleges throughout Great Britain, and
a member movement of the International Fellowship of Evangelical Students. For
more information about local and national activities write to UCCF, 38 De
Montfort Street, Leicester LE1 7GP, email us at email@uccf.org.uk, or visit the
UCCF website at www.uccf.org.uk.

To Nigel's son, Jacob, and
Andrew's godson, Eden Dean.
That they would grow up
loving God's word.

Contents

Foreword

I have been waiting for this book for years. I had even thought of trying to write it myself. The need for a straightforward, user-friendly guide to how to read the Bible was obvious. There were plenty of learned studies for pastors and theologians, but very little that I could confidently put in the hands of the average Christian wanting help in understanding the Bible for himself or herself or in teaching it to others.

But I kept putting off writing the book. It seeming impossible to make the task of handling Scripture both accessible and interesting. Now, to my great relief, I won't have to try. Nigel Beynon and Andrew Sach have brilliantly succeeded. They have made available all the basic tools we need to open up the meaning of Scripture, and they have done so in a fresh, engaging style that is simple, but never simplistic; thorough, but never dull. This book will help all who read and apply it, and those who teach it, to hear the authentic word of God in the Scriptures. Nothing is more important for the churches and the world today.

Vaughan Roberts
Rector of St Ebbe's Church, Oxford

Acknowledgments

Andrew would like to thank his Bible study group at St Helen's and friends from Taunton 2 summer camp, who served as guinea pigs for prototypes of the toolkit. Andrew wrote part of his contribution while studying for a semester at Moore College in Sydney and he is grateful to everyone there who provided encouragement, especially as the publisher's deadline drew close ('nearly my worst essay crisis ever!')

Nigel would like to thank many of the church family at St Helen's and a bunch of students at Word Alive who were introduced to these tools in talks and seminars. He also thanks his wife, Elisa, for letting him interrupt many mealtimes with musings about this book.

It was Brian O'Donoghue at St Helen's who first suggested that this book should be written. Lots of people at IVP, but in particular our editors Sandra Byatt and Eleanor Trotter, have helped the project along. Ed Shaw took the toolkit for a test-drive at his church in Bristol and has kindly written about the experience in the Appendix.

Roo Standring introduced us to the Power Team; Mark Ashton told us the joke about the parting of the Red Sea; William Taylor came up with the plastic-cup analogy; we could go on.

We acknowledge that much of the material in this book was first taught to us by others, those 'on whose shoulders we stand'. They showed us how to feed ourselves from God's Word, and we are deeply indebted to them.

Most of all, we render praises to our heavenly Father, who by his Spirit has inspired the Holy Scriptures, which have made us 'wise for salvation through faith in Christ Jesus' (2 Timothy 3:15). To him be all the glory!

Nigel Beynon
Andrew Sach
July 2005

Introduction

'It's all a matter of interpretation'

Most conversations I've had with non-Christians about the Bible end up there sooner or later. It's all a matter of interpretation. Sure, *you* say it means that Jesus is God and that sex outside marriage is wrong and that heaven is only for Christians, but maybe for *me* it means that Jesus was just a good teacher and sex with anyone is OK as long as you both want it and heaven is for everybody. It's all just a matter of interpretation.

Actually, we've all been conditioned to think like that. It's part of the whole philosophical movement called 'postmodernism', and over the last few decades it has infiltrated the TV shows that we watch and the classrooms that we sit in. Postmodernism teaches that when I come to a piece of literature such as the Bible, what matters is not what it means, but what it means *for me*. And that might be different from what it means *for you*. And that's OK.

I wonder if you've ever been in a Bible study like this:

Leader Does anyone have any thoughts about verse 1?
Person A I think it's talking about X, and ... (blah, blah) ...
Person B Yes, I see what you're saying, Person A, and I totally

respect you. For me, though, it means *Y*, the opposite of *X*.

Leader   Mmmm. Thank you both. Let's move on to verse 2.

That's postmodernism in action. The text means one thing for one person and the complete opposite for another, but both interpretations are to be respected and treated as equally valid.

But the apostle Paul doesn't see it like that. He thinks that there is a right and a wrong way to understand the Bible. He writes to a young church leader:

> Do your best to present yourself to God as one approved, a workman who does not need to be ashamed and who correctly handles the word of truth.
> (2 Timothy 2:15)

Here are some of the joys of understanding the Bible correctly:

- You hear the voice of your heavenly Father speaking to you.
- You learn what he is really like from his own lips (and often God's true character turns out to be a surprise because we're so used to second-hand caricatures).
- You discover the wonderful truth of salvation, and how to be sure of heaven.
- You find out the things that are on God's heart, what really matters to him about this world and his will for your life.
- The truth actually changes you – get this, it doesn't just inform you of things, it *does* things in you.

On the flip side, the consequences of *mis*understanding the Bible can be devastating:

> He [Paul] writes the same way in all his letters, speaking in them of these matters. His letters contain some things that are hard to understand, which ignorant and unstable

people distort, as they do the other Scriptures, to their own destruction.
(2 Peter 3:16)

I know that after I leave, savage wolves will come in among you and will not spare the flock. Even from your own number men will arise and distort the truth in order to draw away disciples after them. So be on your guard! Remember that for three years I never stopped warning each of you night and day with tears.
(Acts 20:29–31)

Many of the world's leading cults – Mormonism, Jehovah's Witnesses, Christian Science – claim to place the Bible at the centre of their religion. They just interpret it 'differently'. But even mainstream Christians can end up in a real mess because they think that the Bible is saying or promising something that it isn't. I (Andrew) think of a Christian I knew at university who was young but dying of cancer. Some well-meaning Christians told her mum that she would be healed if only they had 'enough faith'. It was a desperately cruel error; they added the agonizing guilt of 'maybe I haven't believed enough' to the grief of losing a daughter. But they had verses in the Bible – tragically misunderstood verses – to back it up.

The truth is that without some care in your interpretation, you can make the Bible say almost anything. It may shock you, for example, to discover that the Bible says twice that 'there is no God'. Check it out – Psalms 14:1 and 53:1. Seriously, have a look. Or if you're a single bloke and wondering whether you should get married, then the Old Testament has clear guidance for you: 'you shall go out with joy' (Isaiah 55:12, NKJV). If you know a girl by that name, you're on to a winner.

In our work with university students in London, we've seen people get the Bible right and watched their eyes light up with excitement at new truths and seen their lives changed by the word of God. It's been a privilege to witness that. But we've also seen people get the Bible wrong and end up in trouble or even losing their faith altogether. And that breaks our hearts. That's why we've written this book.

This is a book to help you to understand the Bible correctly. We don't claim that we will always get it perfectly right. But nearly right is more valuable than half right and much better than wholly wrong.

We want to help you to dig deeper to find hidden riches in the Bible. We hope that parts of the Bible that previously have seemed like gobbledegook will begin to make sense, and that bits that were clear already will become even more vivid and gripping.

Most of all, we want to help you to do all this *for yourself*. You may go to a church where the pastor is a gifted teacher of the Bible, and each week he brings it alive for you. Certainly there are many useful commentaries written by scholars who understand the Bible very well, and explain it verse by verse (see p. 158 for some recommendations). Pastors and scholars are a gift from God, and we should be grateful for their help. But we shouldn't be content to leave it entirely to the experts. The Bereans in the book of Acts are an example to us, because even though they were taught by the great apostle Paul himself, they nonetheless 'examined the Scriptures every day to see if what Paul said was true' (Acts 17:11).

The book is based on the idea of a toolkit. Sorry if that conjures up painful memories of failed DIY projects, or hours waiting for a mechanic on the hard shoulder of the motorway. There aren't any spanners or screwdrivers here, but a set of practical tools to help you get to the bottom of any Bible passage. We'll look at things like context, repetition, linking words, different translations and more.

A science and an art

Reading the Bible is both a science and an art. By calling it a science, we mean that as a discipline it is rigorous and structured:

there are certain principles to follow in order to understand the Bible correctly. Those are what we hope to teach in the following pages.

However, we don't want you to get the idea that understanding the Bible is an automatic and mechanical process – as though you just apply the tools and out pops the answer. It's not like that.

Understanding the Bible is also an art. It is something you learn by doing, something you 'catch' as well as get taught, something intuitive as much as logical. That is why we have called the following chapters 'tools' rather than 'rules' – like a master craftsman, you will need to exercise judgment and skill in the way that you use them.

Bear the following points in mind:

- You won't need every tool for every passage you read.
- Some tools will be crucial for some passages, others secondary.
- Sometimes the tools will work only when used together, one tool enabling you to use another.

Rather like learning to ride a bike, after a while you will forget the tools because the principles behind them have become second nature.

The format of this book

Each chapter introduces you to a separate tool and explains how it works. Although there are illustrations from the Bible throughout, we'll sometimes spend a bit longer on a 'Worked example' to show you how that particular tool really can help us discover something exciting and relevant that the Bible is saying. Finally, the 'Dig deeper!' exercises give you a chance to practise using the tools for yourself.

At the end we've included a brief appendix with a suggestion of how you might use the 'toolkit' concept in your small group.

A note on authorship. This book was very much a joint effort – we planned it together, wrote about half of it each, and then revised and edited each other's chapters. Most of the time we write as 'we', but we had to use 'I' for anecdotes that only happened to one of us, or (in the case of Nigel) when referring to 'my wife Elisa'.

What the Bible Is and How We Should Approach It

Before we jump in with our first tool, we're going to pause to examine the nature of the Bible – what kind of book it is, and how it came about. That will lead us to the right way to approach it.

Imagine that a friend who isn't a Christian asks you, 'Why do you bother reading the Bible? Isn't it out of date?' How would you respond?

We hope you would disagree. The Bible isn't like an old railway timetable that has outlived its usefulness because things have changed. It is something that the eternal, almighty God has said, and therefore it is relevant and important for all times and cultures: 'The grass withers and the flowers fall, but the word of our God stands for ever' (Isaiah 40:8).

You can see where your friend is coming from, though. We would have to admit that parts of the Bible seem a bit 'dated'. After all, it was written between 2,000 and 3,500 years ago; it describes the history and events of people we've never heard of and who often don't seem anything like us; it talks about what food you should and shouldn't eat, how you should sacrifice animals, and the type of material you should make your clothes from, none of which applies to us today. It isn't hard to see why someone might say it's out of date.

Our dilemma is caused by the dual nature of the Bible. It is a *divine book*, spoken by God, and therefore it is always true and relevant. And yet at the same time it is a *human book*, written by people a long time ago, and therefore it is in some senses 'dated'. Let's think about each of these two natures of the Bible and how they should influence the way that we approach it.

A divine book

By calling it a 'divine book', we mean simply that the Bible comes directly from God. Behind the various human authors, he is the ultimate author.

That's a huge claim to make, and lots of people would dispute it. But for Christians the issue is settled very easily: this is what Jesus himself believed about the Bible.

When asked by the Pharisees about divorce, Jesus said this: 'Haven't you read ... that at the beginning the Creator "made them male and female", and said, "For this reason a man will leave his father and mother and be united to his wife, and the two will become one flesh"?' (Matthew 19:4–5).

Jesus quotes from Genesis 2:24, which, he says, was spoken by 'the Creator'. But when we turn to Genesis 2:24, we find that it is not a direct pronouncement from God (compare 2:18), but simply part of the narrative written by the human author of Genesis, probably Moses. However, Jesus sees this human sentence as something spoken by the Creator, God himself. We could multiply the examples showing that this is typical of Jesus' attitude to the Old Testament.

The apostle Paul delivers the same verdict: 'All Scripture is God-breathed' (2 Timothy 3:16).

You can't speak without breathing – your lips move, but there will be no sound (try it!). Words travel on our breath. That explains what Paul is saying about the Old Testament ('Scripture'). It comes out of God's mouth. It is his word. This is sometimes called the doctrine of *inspiration*.

But what about the New Testament? That was written after Jesus returned to heaven, so presumably we can't know what he thought about it. Wrong. While Jesus was on earth he told his apostles that they were to be his witnesses and speak for him after he had left (see John 15:27; 17:20), and they went on to write the books and letters we call the New Testament. In effect, Jesus deliberately planned and commissioned the New Testament. To make sure they got it right, he didn't just leave the apostles to write it by themselves. He promised the help of his Spirit: 'I have much more to say to you, more than you can now bear. But when he, the Spirit of truth, comes, he will guide you into all truth. He will not speak on his own; he will speak only what he hears, and he will tell you what is yet to come. He will bring glory to me by taking from what is mine and making it known to you' (John 16:12–14).

The other New Testament writers seem conscious of this. Peter, for instance, wrote: 'Dear friends, this is now my second letter to you. I have written both of them as reminders to stimulate you to wholesome thinking. I want you to recall the words spoken in the past by the holy prophets and the command given by our Lord and Saviour through your apostles' (2 Peter 3:1–2).

Do you see what Peter is saying? It is *Jesus'* command, but from the apostles' lips. The apostles speak for God.

Much more could be said about the inspiration of the Bible, but we don't have room here. If you want to take it further, chapter 2 of 📖 *Bible Doctrine* by Wayne Grudem (IVP) is highly recommended.

Let's think about four implications that flow from the Bible being a divine book.

The Bible is alive, not dead history

If the Bible is God's word, then, far from being 'out of date', it is a book that is alive and speaks to us today. As the book of Hebrews puts it: 'the word of God is living and active. Sharper than any double-edged sword, it penetrates even to dividing soul and spirit, joints and marrow; it judges the thoughts and attitudes of the heart' (Hebrews 4:12).

Imagine a lawyer who has to answer a tricky legal question. He knows that the answer lies in the dusty, leather-bound volumes in the law library, among all the previous cases and legal precedents. However, reading those books is rather boring and takes a long time. It's much easier to phone up a fellow lawyer who knows more than he does. His friend can tell him the answer straight away; it's quick and easy.

Of course, our lawyer friend still thinks highly of the books in the law library. They are the final authority on what is right and wrong. But he goes to read them only when he really has to, or when he needs to check that his friend's answer is right. Otherwise, it's much easier to stick with the immediate answer he gets over the phone.

That can sum up how many of us treat the Bible. We have lots of questions we want God to answer, but we think of the Bible as rather old and boring. It's much easier to try and get answers more directly. We either ask God to tell us answers in some way that doesn't involve the Bible, or we ask Christian friends for their opinion. We still think the Bible is very important, though. Like the law library, it is our final authority; it decides what is right and wrong. But we go there only as a last resort, to check on things we've heard from elsewhere.

From what we've said about the Bible, we hope you can see that that is a huge misunderstanding! The Bible isn't like a dead law book, true but boring. It is God's word. It is what God is saying today. It is living and active. It is like speaking to the friend on the phone, only the friend is God himself.

It would be good to keep this in mind every time we sit down and open the Bible. Banish any thoughts of a boring library, and think instead of picking up the phone and discovering your Creator on the other end of the line. God is speaking. That is really what is happening as we read the Bible.

The Bible is true and doesn't make mistakes

One of the wonderful things about God is that he doesn't lie (Titus 1:2). He doesn't make mistakes either, because he knows everything that there is to know. If the Bible is God's word, then it follows that the Bible doesn't lie or make mistakes. No wonder that Jesus can say to God his Father: 'Sanctify them by the truth; your word is truth' (John 17:17).

We can trust everything that the Bible says. It will never mislead us – so long as we understand it correctly, that is.

Yes, we know that the Catholic Church persecuted Galileo because its leaders were convinced from the Bible that the sun orbited the earth: 'The sun rises and the sun sets, and hurries back to where it rises' (Ecclesiastes 1:5). 'Ha!' says the sceptic. 'How hopelessly naïve of the pre-scientific Bible writers, who knew nothing of cosmology! The Bible must be riddled with mistakes like that.' But of course we still speak of 'sunrise' in our own day. That's what it looks like from the standpoint of someone on earth. It's not saying anything about cosmology. It's not a mistake.

The word of God is the surest foundation that you can build your life on.

We can understand the word of God only by the Spirit of God

Consider these verses:

However, as it is written:

'No eye has seen,
   no ear has heard,
no mind has conceived
   what God has prepared for those who love him' –

but God has revealed it to us by his Spirit.

The Spirit searches all things, even the deep things of God. For who among men knows the thoughts of a man except the man's spirit within him? In the same way no-one

knows the thoughts of God except the Spirit of God. We have not received the spirit of the world but the Spirit who is from God, that we may understand what God has freely given us.
(1 Corinthians 2:9–12)

Paul's point is clear: we need God's Spirit to understand God's word. Given that it was the Spirit who inspired it in the first place, that comes as no surprise. There's another implication, though:

The man without the Spirit does not accept the things that come from the Spirit of God, for they are foolishness to him, and he cannot understand them, because they are spiritually discerned.
(1 Corinthians 2:14)

Someone who isn't a Christian (i.e. the 'man [or woman] without the Spirit') won't be able fully to understand the Bible, however many qualifications or degrees in theology he or she may have. We should be wary of the 'expert' on television, or the professor who's written the latest controversial book about Christianity. It's easy to bow to what seems to be impressive knowledge, but if they haven't got the Spirit of God working in them, then they haven't a hope of grasping the Bible's message.

On the other hand, everyone who is a Christian *can* understand the Bible for themselves, since all Christians have the Spirit. The role of our pastor or minister is not to tell us private secrets to which they alone have access, but to point us to the verses in front of us so that we see for ourselves what the Bible is saying. This is very liberating and exciting – all God's children have access to God's truth.

Yet we need continually to express our dependence on God for a right understanding of him and his ways. He is the one who grants insight (2 Timothy 2:7; Philippians 3:15). And so we must pray. Pray before you open the Bible. Pray when you get stuck and don't understand. Pray again when you do understand it – say thank you! Pray, pray, pray!

It is vital that we remember this. In the rest of this book we are going to concentrate on what we might call 'our part' in understanding the Bible, as opposed to 'God's part' of enabling us to understand. However, we would hate you to get the impression that just because we spend most time on 'our part', we think God's part isn't very important. Not at all! Better than any of the tools that we will learn about later is the privilege of prayer. If the Bible is God speaking to us down the telephone, then prayer is our way of speaking back – 'I don't get it. Please help me see what you mean'; 'I'm struggling to accept what you're saying, Father. Please help me to trust you'; 'This is amazing, Lord. I praise you for what you are showing me.'

What God says goes
The fourth implication of the Bible's being God's word comes from remembering who God is. He is the supreme Lord and King of the universe. He is the one in charge. Given that, it should be obvious that what he says goes.

This is sometimes called the *authority* of the Bible. It carries the same authority as the God who speaks it and so has the right to say what is true and to demand obedience. As Christians we want to live with God in charge of us, and in practice that means living in submission to the words of Scripture. Listening to Jesus' voice and following him in all that he says is a matter of instinct: 'My sheep listen to my voice; I know them, and they follow me' (John 10:27).

Yet, even with God's Spirit working in us, we still have a sinful nature, and that part of us doesn't want to listen to God or obey him (Galatians 5:17). The simple fact that the New Testament letters contain so many rebukes and commands about what we should and shouldn't do is ample testimony to the fact that living with God in charge doesn't come easily to us.

Earlier we quoted part of a statement by Paul about the Bible being God-breathed. Here it is in full:

All Scripture is God-breathed and is useful for teaching, rebuking, correcting and training in righteousness.
(2 Timothy 3:16)

Paul expects the Bible to tell us off when we are getting things wrong, and to correct us where we are veering off course. As we read the Bible we should expect to find God saying things we don't like or find difficult. We should expect to be rebuked and corrected.

When that happens, it is really important that we accept what God says. When some people read what the Bible teaches about predestination, or homosexuality, or wives submitting to their husbands (to pick three controversial examples), they respond by saying, 'I can't accept that', or 'Surely we must interpret this in a different way.' Now, of course, it's very important to ask whether the Bible really *does* say what we think it does – that is what this book is going to help us with. But once we are clear about what the Bible says, the question is whether we will accept what it says.

Part of us does want to hear and follow what God says, but part of us doesn't. We should harbour a little self-suspicion: just because we don't like what we are reading doesn't mean we've got it wrong; in fact it might very well mean we've got it right!

A human book

Having thought about the Bible as a divine book, let's turn now to the other side of the coin – that it is a human book also.

We hardly need to prove that the Bible is a human book. That's obvious as soon as we start to read it. For example, Philippians 1:1 tells us that this part of the Bible was written by a man called Paul; from the way he writes it is clearly what we would call a letter; it is addressed to Christians in a place called Philippi. It is clearly a 'human' document.

Often, the human authors give us some personal information about themselves and their involvement with what they are writing:

I, Daniel, was exhausted and lay ill for several days. Then I got up and went about the king's business. I was appalled by the vision; it was beyond understanding.
(Daniel 8:27)

The man who saw it has given testimony, and his testimony is true. He knows that he tells the truth, and he testifies so that you also may believe.
(John 19:35)

The words of the Teacher, son of David, king of Jerusalem . . .
(Ecclesiastes 1:1)

There is a right sense to saying the Bible is 'dated': not that it is no longer relevant, but that it was written a long time ago. This is sometimes called historical *particularity* – the Bible is written by particular people, at a particular time, in a particular place, for a particular reason. Their humanity comes through. Their particular circumstances come through. That's why you find verses in the Bible like this: 'When you come, bring the cloak that I left with Carpus at Troas, and my scrolls, especially the parchments' (2 Timothy 4:13). If you go hunting in this verse for God's special message for you, you'll be barking up the wrong tree. It is particular to the human writer Paul, who was beginning to get cold as winter approached and needed his overcoat!

So then, the Bible is a human document. That doesn't overturn what we said earlier about God speaking to us in the Bible; that is all still true. But the *way* God speaks to us is through *human* authors. They weren't mindless robots, writing as God dictated from above. Rather, God worked through them as people, preserving their personality, literary style and culture, yet at the same time guiding them by his Spirit so that they always wrote his eternal truth.

This all means that we have some work to do. We must work at understanding the different writers correctly, exploring their situations, their purpose in writing, how they have expressed themselves. As we do that, we will come to know God's voice in our lives. That is what the following tools are going to help us do.

What we have learnt in this chapter
Understanding the nature of the Bible leads us to the right way to approach it. It is a divine book, the very word of God. That means that it is

- living and active today
- utterly true and reliable
- understood only with the help of the Spirit
- the ultimate authority for Christians

But at the same time it is a human book, written by real people in real situations. We need to work hard at understanding it. We need *tools*! Read on!

2

The Author's Purpose Tool

When I (Nigel) was a student I remember leading a Bible study on the following verses:

> [God] has saved us and called us to a holy life – not because of anything we have done but because of his own purpose and grace. This grace was given us in Christ Jesus before the beginning of time, but it has now been revealed through the appearing of our Saviour, Christ Jesus, who has destroyed death and has brought life and immortality to light through the gospel.
> (2 Timothy 1:9–10)

As I led the discussion, I got the group to look at all the exciting gospel truths that Paul mentions – we are saved by grace and not works (we spent some time on that because I thought it was great); God chooses us before time; Jesus has defeated death; holiness is important, etc. I asked questions about each of these topics and we thought about the implications for our lives. However, there was one question that I never asked. *Why does Paul say all this?*

I spent all our time concentrating on *what* Paul said, but we didn't think about *why*.

It sounds obvious when you say it, but the Bible authors wrote their books with a particular purpose in mind. They weren't just scribbling down random things that popped into their heads. We know that, because often they tell us what their aim is. For instance, near the end of his Gospel John says: 'Jesus did many other miraculous signs in the presence of his disciples, which are not written in this book. But these are written so that you may believe that Jesus is the Christ, the Son of God, and that by believing you may have life in his name' (John 20:30–31).

There are lots of things that John could have told us about but hasn't. He has selected his material with the *particular aim* of showing us that Jesus is the Christ, the Son of God, so that we will come to believe in him and so have life.

Since the biblical writers were inspired, their purpose is God's purpose. That means that one of the biggest and most helpful questions we can ever ask of a passage in the Bible is simply, 'Why did the author write this?' If we glean one or two insights along the way, but miss the overall purpose of what they are saying, then we haven't really understood them at all.

That was the error I fell into with my student Bible study described above. I focused on many individual truths in the passage, and we learnt a lot, but I overlooked the overall thrust, the big point. You might say that I missed the wood for the trees.

'This is why I am writing . . . '

Sometimes the author explicitly tells us why he is writing his book, in what we might call his 'purpose statement'. We've already seen one from John's Gospel. Here are two more examples:

> Many have undertaken to draw up an account of the things that have been fulfilled among us, just as they were handed down to us by those who from the first were eye-witnesses and servants of the word. Therefore, since I myself have

carefully investigated everything from the beginning, it seemed good also to me to write an orderly account for you, most excellent Theophilus, so that you may know the certainty of the things you have been taught.
(Luke 1:1–4)

I write these things to you who believe in the name of the Son of God so that you may know that you have eternal life.
(1 John 5:13)

If the author has told us why he is writing, we should let that guide our interpretation of the rest of the book.

The letter of 1 John, for example, contains several 'tests' by which you can find out whether your faith is genuine. Do you trust that Jesus is King? Do you have a genuine love for other Christians? Is your life marked by obedience to Jesus' commands?

They are great questions, but sometimes in the hands of people with over-sensitive consciences they can wreak havoc. One of the most loving Christians we know has regular 1 John crises, thinking that he's failed the loving-people test and so he can't be a real Christian. But he would do well to look again at the purpose statement of 1 John (see above). It is a letter written to believers to assure them, and to give them confidence that they have eternal life. You're supposed to think, 'I love other Christians – not perfectly, but I do love them – and that's fantastic because it means I must be a real Christian on my way to heaven!' Using 1 John to *undermine* your assurance is like using a kettle to make ice-cubes – it's the opposite of what it was designed to do.

Let's play detective

In the absence of a specific 'purpose statement' from our author, we need to play detective – hunting through the book for clues about why it has been written and what its main themes are. Familiarity is the key, and nothing beats reading the whole thing several times. However, we recognize that that's a somewhat more realistic prospect for Philemon or 3 John than for a fifty-chapter epic like Genesis!

If you're dealing with either a New Testament letter or an Old Testament prophet (e.g. Jeremiah) the following questions might be helpful.

- Who is writing and to whom?
- What is the situation of the author and of the readers?
- Are we made aware of any problems that need to be addressed?
- Are there any repeated themes, or a single idea that holds everything together?

When it comes to a narrative, you can get some idea of the author's purpose from what he chooses to put in and what he leaves out of his account. The Old Testament deals with hundreds of years of history. Sometimes the writer hits the accelerator pedal and covers someone's whole life in one or two verses; at other times he slows down and gives us a few hours in great detail. We should be asking, 'Why do we hear so much about this and so little about that?'

We should always be reaching for the Author's Purpose tool when we come to two different accounts of the same events. Much of the storyline of the books of Samuel and Kings is repeated in Chronicles, but they don't include quite the same things or share exactly the same emphases. The Chronicler leaves out David's adultery with Bathsheba, for example – that is because his purpose is to celebrate what is best about the kings of Judah, in preparation for the greatest king of all, Jesus. The second book of Samuel keeps it in. He has a different purpose, namely to show us that even King David is a sinner in need of a Saviour.

Matthew, Mark and Luke record many of the same incidents in Jesus' life, and to a lesser extent they overlap with John. But beware: it may be a mistake when reading Matthew to cross-reference to Luke's version of the same story and fill in missing details from what Luke tells us. What if Matthew *meant* for those details to be missing? What if he deliberately put the emphasis in a different place? What if his *purpose* was different from Luke's?

We've told you how to play detective with letters, prophecy and narrative. What about other books, like Ecclesiastes or Leviticus or the Song of Songs? The answer is that it's more difficult, and sadly we can only offer that traditional piece of sleuthing advice: follow your nose. What themes dominate? What seem to be the author's concerns?

The Author's Purpose tool and the other tools

Author's Purpose is king. It is the tool *par excellence*, the Swiss army knife from which all of the other tools fold out, and which keeps them all together. In some ways, the whole point of having a Repetition tool or a Linking Words tool or any other tool is to help you to get a hold of the Author's Purpose. Never forget it!

Worked example

Since we've already mentioned 2 Timothy, let's return to that. It's a short enough letter to be read and reread several times. As we play detective, the following picture emerges.

Paul is writing to Timothy, with whom he has a close relationship (1:1–7). Paul is an apostle, a commissioned spokesperson for Christ (1:1, 11). As a result of his gospel preaching he has suffered greatly (1:11, 12; 3:10, 11). He is in prison (1:8) and has been deserted by many (1:15; 4:14–16). He thinks that he is about die (4:6–8).

Timothy is a church leader (1:6; 2:2, 14). There are false teachers in his church who are distorting the true gospel (2:14–18, 22–26; 3:1–10, 13). Worse still, some in the church are keen to hear these false ideas (4:3–4).

Paul spends most of his time encouraging Timothy to stand for the true gospel (1:8, 13, 14), to teach it himself and train others to teach it also (2:2, 15; 3:14–17). He warns Timothy of the false teachers and instructs him how to deal with them (2:14–26; 3:1–10). He tells Timothy throughout that he must endure suffering (1:8; 2:3–13; 3:10–12). He continually reminds Timothy of the future – both the reward of heaven (e.g. 1:1, 10; 2:10; 4:8) and the sobering reality of judgment (2:12–13; 4:1).

Putting it all together, our detective work suggests that Paul's purpose in writing to Timothy is *to urge him to continue to stand for the true gospel despite the suffering that it will bring, in light of the glorious future that awaits him.*

With that in mind, let's return to the two verses I mentioned at the start:

> [God] has saved us and called us to a holy life – not because of anything we have done but because of his own purpose and grace. This grace was given us in Christ Jesus before the beginning of time, but it has now been revealed through the appearing of our Saviour, Christ Jesus, who has destroyed death and has brought life and immortality to light through the gospel.
>
> (2 Timothy 1:9–10)

It's merely a description of the Christian gospel. That's strange, because Timothy already knows the gospel. It's not news to him that he's been saved, or called to a holy life; there's nothing novel in the idea that Jesus has destroyed death. It's all familiar stuff. It's the same old gospel.

The same old gospel. Exactly. Given what we now know about the purpose of the letter, it all makes sense. Stick with the gospel, Timothy. The same old gospel. Keep on teaching it, even though people in your church don't always want to hear it, even though it's going to mean suffering and hardship. This is the gospel, Timothy – God has saved us! Not because of what we have done but because of his grace! Jesus has defeated death, Timothy! Life and immortality are ahead of us. Isn't that fantastic? Isn't it worth suffering for?

Paul reminds Timothy of the gospel to encourage him to stand by it, whatever people may do to him. And what an encouragement it is for us to do the same.

DIG DEEPER!

Read 1 Corinthians 13 on its own and then think about what it means. Write down the main points you think the passage is making.

Time to play detective. Look up the following verses to get a feel for some of the issues that prompted Paul to write to Corinth: 1:10–12; 3:1–4; 4:6–10; 6:1, 6–8; 11:17–18.

How do they make you read chapter 13 differently?

3
The Context Tool

What is the difference between a novel and an encyclopaedia? Well, the encyclopaedia is certainly heavier, unless you read very long novels! But what about how you read them?

When you use the encyclopaedia you simply turn to the entry you are interested in, say 'Asparagus'. The fact that the entry before 'Asparagus' was on 'Asps' (cobras) and the one after it was on 'Aspartame' (an artificial sweetener) is irrelevant. In fact, you don't even look at them, unless you get bored with reading about asparagus.

Imagine reading a novel in the same way: you open the book up halfway through, and read the third paragraph down. Try it if you like. We can guarantee it won't make much sense. You don't know who the characters are or how the plot is unfolding; you have no idea what is going on. That is why we read a novel from beginning to end.

Which of these two approaches should we use when we read the Bible?

We should treat it more like the novel. Not that we have to read the whole thing from beginning to end every time we open it. But we do need to recognize that individual chapters are connected to what comes before and after. Context matters! In fact, as someone has said, *a text without a context is a con.* You have a minimal chance of understanding it correctly.

I remember hearing someone introduce a song with these words from John: 'But I, when I am lifted up from the earth, will draw all men to myself' (John 12:32). Then they said something like, 'We are now are going to lift Jesus up on our praises, and as we do that he will draw people to himself.' That was an example of the encyclopaedia method. It completely ignored the very next sentence: ' "But I, when I am lifted up from the earth, will draw all men to myself." He said this to show the kind of death he was going to die' (John 12:32–33).

Jesus' talk of being 'lifted up' speaks of his being lifted up on the cross; that is how he will draw all men to himself. It has nothing to do with our praises. Of course, this doesn't diminish the value of praising Jesus in song. Indeed, we should encourage each other to do so. We just shouldn't use John 12:32 for that purpose.

There are different levels of context (see figure 1). A sentence comes in the context of a paragraph. A paragraph comes in the context of a chapter or section. A chapter comes in the context of a whole Bible book. Lastly, the book comes in the context of

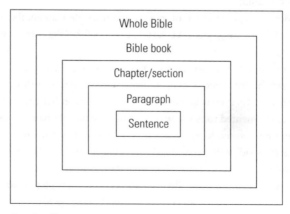

Figure 1. Levels of context

the whole Bible – but that's something that we'll look at separately using the Bible Timeline tool.

It is very important that, as we study any part of the Bible, we ask how it fits with what comes before and after. For instance, in Exodus 20:3 we read, 'You shall have no other gods before me.'

This is, of course, the first of the Ten Commandments. If we read this and the nine others that follow it *on their own*, it might be possible to arrive at a kind of legalism – the idea that you become one of God's people by being good enough, that you must earn your way to heaven by perfectly keeping all the rules.

That terrible misunderstanding is impossible, however, if we start reading just one verse earlier: 'I am the LORD your God, who brought you out of Egypt, out of the land of slavery. You shall have no other gods before me' (Exodus 20:2–3).

God gives these commandments to a people that he has *already* saved from Egypt – that's clear not only from the preceding verse, but also from the context of the previous nineteen chapters, which have described the rescue. God can't be saying they have to obey his laws *in order to be* saved. He's saying that this is how they should behave *now that they have been* saved.

Worked example

The book of 2 Samuel is full of tragedy and tears. Be warned, the next couple of pages are going to be very sad. We pick up the sorry tale in chapter 13.

Scene 1: King David's son Amnon rapes his half-sister, Tamar. Afterwards he hates her. 'Get up and get out,' he says. 'Get this woman out of here.' And it ends in tears. 'Tamar put ashes on her head and tore the ornamented robe she was wearing. She put her hand on her head and went away, weeping aloud as she went' (2 Samuel 13:19).

Scene 2: David's other son, Absalom, arranges for the murder of his half-brother Amnon, to avenge his sister. At the news of Amnon's death, there are more tears: 'the king's sons came in, wailing loudly. The king, too, and all his servants wept very bitterly' (2 Samuel 13:36).

But in chapter 15 things get worse still. Not just rape. Not just murder. Civil war. Absalom has pretensions to the throne. He is pretty good-looking, we're told, and a very smooth operator. Whenever anyone goes to visit his father, the king, Absalom intercepts them and turns on the charm. In this way he steals the hearts of the men of Israel.

Eventually Absalom secretly declares himself king in his father's place. David has to flee for his life. He leaves the palace behind, he leaves ten of his wives. (Absalom later rapes them.) He leaves behind his countrymen. It's a pretty unhappy procession: 'The whole countryside wept aloud as all the people passed by . . . David continued up the Mount of Olives, weeping as he went; his head was covered and he was barefoot. All the people with him covered their heads too and were weeping as they went up' (2 Samuel 15:23, 30).

Finally, the civil war is over, and David's army wins. Absalom's hair is so long that it gets stuck in a tree as he's riding along on his horse. As he dangles in the air, Joab puts a spear through him. A mighty victory. David's life is no longer in danger. The rebel Absalom is crushed. Fantastic.

But that's not quite how David took the news:

> The king was shaken. He went up to the room over the gateway and wept. As he went, he said: 'O my son Absalom! My son, my son Absalom! If only I had died instead of you – O Absalom, my son, my son!'
>
> Joab was told, 'The king is weeping and mourning for Absalom.' And for the whole army the victory that day was turned into mourning, because on that day the troops heard it said, 'The king is grieving for his son' . . . The king covered his face and cried aloud, 'O my son Absalom! O Absalom, my son, my son!'
> (2 Samuel 18:33 – 19:4)

It is a catalogue of tragedy for David. Rape, murder, civil war, the death of a son he loved despite everything. I don't know about you, but I find myself choking up at some of the verses I've quoted. It's just so desperate.

But why does it happen? Why so much suffering? Why such unimaginable sorrow? So many tears?

As we've reported it above, it makes no sense. If you pick up the story from chapter 13 (as we have done), it is meaningless. But the story doesn't begin in chapter 13. We need the context.

Chapter 11 of 2 Samuel narrates some events that we're more familiar with. King David is walking on the roof of his palace, and he catches sight of a beautiful woman named Bathsheba taking a bath. She's a real stunner – he can't keep his eyes off her. Turns out she's married to someone else, but that doesn't stop David, and he sleeps with her. Unfortunately she gets pregnant, and the only way to cover it up is to get her husband killed in battle.

But the cover-up fails, because there is a witness who sees everything. God sees it. And it displeases him. And through his prophet Nathan, he speaks these terrifying words:

> 'Why did you despise the word of the LORD by doing what is evil in his eyes? You struck down Uriah the Hittite with the sword and took his wife to be your own. You killed him with the sword of the Ammonites. Now, therefore, the sword shall never depart from your house, because you despised me and took the wife of Uriah the Hittite to be your own.'
>
> (2 Samuel 12:9–10)

All the tragedy of the following chapters stems from David's sin. 'The sword shall never depart from your house,' God says. And it never does. Rape, murder, civil war, the death of Absalom. All because David turned his back on God and slept with Bathsheba. Who would have thought that the consequences would be so massive?

I don't think we would, would we? We'd never guess that the effects of sin could be so devastating.

It's not the world of the soaps, is it? Or *Friends*? That was a great show, at least the early episodes. Monica, Joey, Chandler, Phoebe,

Rachel, Ross – they don't have much time for Jesus, except as a swearword. But hey, they have a good time, don't they? They have a laugh. They're easy-going. Because rejecting God doesn't matter in *Friends*. It's a world where nothing you do has lasting consequences.

But 2 Samuel is screaming to us, 'That's not the real world. In the real world sin does matter. There are consequences. It wrecks relationships, it messes up lives. It ends in tears. It's not worth it.'

I (Andrew) went to the British Library once. They've got some pretty amazing things there: original Beatles lyrics in John Lennon's handwriting on the backs of envelopes, pages from Leonardo da Vinci's notebook, all kinds of stuff. The thing I liked best was the draft Declaration of War against Germany from the Second World War. It was typed on an old typewriter. And at the top of the page someone had scribbled in pencil, 'To be checked.'

And I thought – no kidding! You'd want to be pretty sure you'd got it right, wouldn't you? You don't want to end up declaring war on Scotland by mistake, because of a typo. The consequences are massive, so you think before you act.

And that is what 2 Samuel would say to us. Think pretty carefully before you turn your back on God. Are you prepared for the consequences?

DIG DEEPER!
Read Mark 8:22–26. What do these verses tell you on their own?

Now look at the context: read verses 14–21 and 27–30. What change is there in the disciples' understanding?

Look at Jesus' description of the problem in 8:18. Has there been another healing miracle alongside the physical one?

4
The Structure Tool

Given what we've said about the importance of context, it's clear that we want to be dealing with whole passages of the Bible rather than with isolated verses. But approaching a great slab of text can be daunting. Where to begin?

A good place to start is to subdivide the passage into smaller, more manageable sections that we can deal with one at a time. Yet at the same time we want to keep the big picture in mind, otherwise we just end up with isolated verses again, and defeat the whole object of tackling a bigger passage in the first place.

The key to looking at the parts without losing sight of the whole (seeing the wood *and* the trees) is to pay attention to the structure of the passage, asking two questions:

1. How has the author broken down his material into sections?
2. How do those sections fit together?

We can apply the Structure tool at different levels. We could use it to divide up a whole book of the Bible into a few major sections (e.g. Isaiah 1 – 39; 40 – 55; 56 – 66), or equally to divide up a small section into even smaller units (e.g. Isaiah 40:1–2, 3–5, 6–8, 9–11). Between two and five sections is probably ideal; any more than that and there will be too many fragments to fit together again easily.

The first stage, then, is to try to discern the way that the *author* wants us to subdivide the passage.

By the way, don't be fooled into thinking that all you have to do is look at the chapter breaks. Chapter and verse numbers aren't divinely inspired; they were added by an editor who was trying to make things easier for us, but occasionally botched it. Unfortunately, the same goes for paragraph breaks and those section titles that the publishers helpfully put in your Bible, which can't always be trusted. It's best to start from scratch, ignoring chapter divisions, ignoring paragraph breaks, ignoring headings. Something we often do is to print out a copy of the passage from the internet (http://www.biblegateway.com) and delete everything except the text itself. That way you start with a clean slate, and it also means that, as you work, you can scribble notes in the margin, use highlighters, underline words, and generally deface it in a way that you might hesitate to do with your Bible.

Sometimes the text itself contains explicit clues about where it breaks up, like those grooves in chocolate bars that show where they snap more easily. For example, the events recounted in John 1:19–51 happen over four days; John splits his narrative into four sections accordingly, using the repeated phrase 'the next day' to alert us to each new subsection (verses 29, 35, 43). Isaiah 40:3–11 can be similarly divided up according to the three different 'voices' that call out.

> A *voice* of one calling:
> 'In the desert prepare
>   the way for the LORD;
> make straight in the wilderness
>   a highway for our God.
> Every valley shall be raised up,
>   every mountain and hill made low;

the rough ground shall become level,
    the rugged places a plain.
And the glory of the LORD will be revealed,
    and all mankind together will see it.
        For the mouth of the LORD has spoken.'

A voice says, 'Cry out.'
    And I said, 'What shall I cry?'
'All men are like grass,
    and all their glory is like the flowers of the field.
The grass withers and the flowers fall,
    because the breath of the LORD blows on them.
    Surely the people are grass.
The grass withers and the flowers fall,
    but the word of our God stands for ever.'

You who bring good tidings to Zion,
    go up on a high mountain.
You who bring good tidings to Jerusalem,
    lift up *your voice* with a shout,
lift it up, do not be afraid;
    say to the towns of Judah,
    'Here is your God!'
See, the Sovereign LORD comes with power,
    and his arm rules for him.
See, his reward is with him,
    and his recompense accompanies him.
He tends his flock like a shepherd.
    He gathers the lambs in his arms
and carries them close to his heart;
    he gently leads those that have young.

In the absence of explicit clues such as those above, we are left
to make sensible judgments, which will depend on what kind of
literature we are dealing with. For a *narrative*, imagine that you

are a film director or a playwright and try to identify the changes of scene. For a *dialogue*, you could break it up according to who is speaking. For one of *Paul's letters*, it might be possible to identify distinct stages in a detailed argument, and to subdivide it that way.

Occasionally the important ideas in a passage are not dealt with *sequentially*, but rather they are woven together throughout the whole thing, like the writing in a stick of seaside rock. In those cases, attempts to force everything into subsections might not be all that profitable; you would be better off tackling the passage *thematically* – identify two or three key topics and consider the whole thing under those headings. It's best to look for sequential divisions first, and to resort to a thematic approach only if that fails.

Having identified your subsections, it is useful to give a title to each one, summing up very briefly what you think it is about. This forces you to pin yourself down and come up with something concrete; you can always change it later.

The second crucial step in using the Structure tool is to work out how your sections fit together. In a letter the different sections might connect together to form a logical argument, while in a narrative the different scenes might contrast with or complement one another. Seeing how the author has structured what he is saying will help us to move towards the unifying big idea of the passage as a whole.

 DIG DEEPER!
Identify the main scenes in John 18:12–27.

What point do you think John might be making by switching back and forth between these two situations?

Bookends and sandwiches

An important structural technique used in the Bible is to put the same phrase at the beginning and end of a section, rather like a pair of bookends. For example, the book of Romans begins and ends like this:

> ... through whom we have received grace and apostleship to bring about the *obedience of faith* for the sake of his name among all the nations ...
> (Romans 1:5, ESV)

> ... but has now been disclosed and through the prophetic writings has been made known to all nations, according to the command of the eternal God, to bring about the *obedience of faith* ...
> (Romans 16:26, ESV)

As well as providing a satisfying poetical symmetry, a pair of bookends signals that everything in between belongs together. That can be a big help when you're trying to divide a book into sections. For example, a major section of the book of Numbers (chapters 27 – 36) is bracketed by two references to the daughters of a man named Zelophehad.

Often there is an important connection between the bookends themselves and what comes in between them. Take this example from the Sermon on the Mount:

> Blessed are the poor in spirit,
>   for theirs is the *kingdom of heaven*.
> Blessed are those who mourn,
>   for they will be comforted.
> Blessed are the meek,
>   for they will inherit the earth.
> Blessed are those who hunger and thirst for righteousness,
>   for they will be filled.

> Blessed are the merciful,
> > for they will be shown mercy.
> Blessed are the pure in heart,
> > for they will see God.
> Blessed are the peacemakers,
> > for they will be called sons of God.
> Blessed are those who are persecuted because of righteousness,
> > for theirs is the *kingdom of heaven*.
> (Matthew 5:3–10)

The bookends, 'kingdom of heaven', show us that the meek, the pure in heart, the peacemakers, etc. aren't just ordinary people who happen to be nice. Rather, they are citizens of the kingdom of heaven. This is a description of kingdom people.

Ezekiel's commissioning as a prophet (2:1 – 3:11) is sandwiched between an amazing vision of God's glory in chapter 1 and a little flashback to that vision in 3:12–13. Again we are invited to consider how these ideas might be linked. It seems that Ezekiel wants to show us that the words he has been given to speak come from none other than the majestic Lord of glory.

This sandwiching together of two different things to emphasize a connection is a favourite technique of Mark's Gospel. For example, the story of Jesus cursing a fig tree outside Jerusalem (Mark 11:12–14, 20–21) is sandwiched together with Jesus' unhappy visit to the temple in Jerusalem (11:15–19). It seems that Jesus' judgment on the fig tree is symbolic of what will happen to the temple, because the religious observance there has become dead and bears no fruit in people's lives.

Chiasm

Can you remember the tale of the three little pigs? The wolf tries to blow down the house of straw, then the house of wood, and finally the house of bricks. It's typical of English stories in that it reaches its climax at the end; we often wait until the last sentence to get the punchline.

However, in Hebrew it's common to put the punchline in the middle of the story. The other sections of the account are then arranged in pairs, in a symmetrical pattern, around that centre. Technically, people call this sort of structure a 'chiasm'. Here is one from the Tower of Babel story in Genesis 11.

Now the whole world
  had one language and a common speech . . .
    they found a plain in Shinar and settled there.
      They said to each other, 'Come, let's make bricks . . . '
        Then they said, 'Come, let us build ourselves a city, with a tower . . .
          But the LORD came down
        to see the city and the tower that the men were building . . .
        The LORD said 'Come, let us go down and confuse . . . '
    it was called Babel – because there
   the LORD confused the language
 of the whole world.

Can you spot the pairs? The 'whole world' is mentioned at the beginning and the end; that's the first. Then the reference to their common 'language' is paired with LORD's acting to confuse their 'language'. Shinar goes with Babel (two names for the same place). 'Build', 'city', 'tower' go with 'build', 'city', 'tower' and so on. Pretty cool, isn't it?

Having identified the chiasm, we can see that the central statement is 'the LORD came down'. That is the turning point for the story. The writer is using this structure to highlight the fact that man's proud conquest is stopped instantly as God intervenes.

The example above works at the level of individual phrases. Daniel 2 – 7, however, contains a huge chiasm at the level of chapters.

> *Chapter 2*: Prophecy of four great kingdoms to come,
> culminating in God's eternal kingdom
>   *Chapter 3*: God saves his people from death
>   (fiery furnace)
>   *Chapter 4*: God is sovereign and deposes kings
>   at will (Nebuchadnezzar)
>   *Chapter 5*: God is sovereign and deposes kings
>   at will (Belshazzar)
>   *Chapter 6*: God saves his people from death
>   (lions)
> *Chapter 7*: Prophecy of four great kingdoms to come,
> culminating in God's eternal kingdom

The structure shows us that the heart of the message of Daniel is that God is sovereign and so he is in charge of his world and of history.

Generally speaking, chiasms are an Old Testament thing, but you do sometimes find them in the New Testament too:

> In the beginning was the Word,
>   and the Word was with God,
>   and the Word was God.
>   He was with God
> in the beginning.
> (John 1:1–2)

Bookends, chiasms or whatever else, the message we hope that we're getting across is that you *must* look at the way the author has structured his material. Lots of the meaning is in the structure.

Worked example

Here is a chiasm from Jonah 1. It will help if you read the whole chapter to get an idea of what is happening.

> *Verse 4*: The LORD hurled a great wind upon the sea
>> *Verse 6*: 'Call out to your god!
>>> *Verse 7*: that we may know on whose account...'
>>>> *Verse 8*: Sailors question Jonah
>>>>> *Verse 9*: 'I fear ...'
>>>>> *Verse 10*: Sailors fear
>>>> *Verse 11*: Sailors question Jonah
>>> *Verse 12*: 'I know that it is on my account' [literally]
>> *Verse 14*: Sailors call to the LORD
> *Verse 15*: The sailors hurl Jonah into the sea
> (ESV)

Once again the key to the whole narrative is found at the centre of the chiasm, in verses 9–10. Here is verse 9:

And he said to them, 'I am a Hebrew, and I fear the LORD, the God of heaven, who made the sea and the dry land.'
(ESV)

Jonah is lying. Not that there's anything wrong with his theology – God is indeed the maker of everything. Jonah is lying about the fact that he 'fears' (i.e. worships) him. Come off it! The rest of the chapter tells us how Jonah has consistently rejected God. He hears the 'word of the LORD' in verses 1–2, but rather than doing what God says he runs away ... by boat! That isn't too bright if you know that God made the sea. There's a terrible storm, and the boat is breaking up and the pagan sailors are all praying their hearts out to whatever god they can think of. The only person who doesn't pray is – Jonah. In fact, he'd rather be thrown overboard and drown than cry out to the God who can help him.

The writer here uses a chiasm (with its punchline in the centre) to highlight Jonah's profession of faith, so we see how much it is at odds with how he actually lives. Jonah is a hypocrite; he might talk a good game when it comes to God, but there is no match-up in his life.

The gulf between Jonah's belief and his behaviour is so wide that you could sail a supertanker through the middle.

It makes us ask awkward questions about ourselves. Do we act as though we believe the things that we say we do? We talk the talk but do we walk the walk, as the saying goes?

Some years ago, a well-known newspaper columnist wrote an article in which he summed up the Christian message pretty accurately, and then he went on:

> If I believed that, or even a tenth of that, how could I care which version of the Prayer Book was used? I would drop my job, sell my house, throw away my possessions, leave my acquaintances and set out into the world with a burning desire to know more. And when I'd found out more, to act upon it and to tell others. Far from being puzzled that Mormons and Adventists should knock at my door, I'm unable to understand how anyone who believes what's written in the Bible could choose to spend his waking hours in any other endeavour.

That gap between belief and behaviour makes no sense.

However, back in Jonah there is another point at the centre of our chiasm, and that's the response of the sailors in verse 10: 'Then the men were exceedingly afraid and said to him, "What is this that you have done?" '

Jonah *says* that he fears God, but the pagans *really* do. They realize that the Creator of the sea and the dry land is not someone you want to mess with. We are told about their fear three times in the chapter (verses 5, 10, 16). But here's a striking thing. When they are about to drown because of the storm, they are just 'afraid'. But when they're *not* about to drown because God has miraculously calmed the sea and it's perfectly safe, they are '*exceedingly* afraid'. In other words, they are more afraid at this breathtaking demonstration of God's power over nature than they are of their own mortality. And they're in good

company; if you know Mark's Gospel, lots of bells will be ringing
(check out Mark 4:35–41).

The idea of fearing God isn't too popular today, because we tend to
think of him more as a kindly Santa Claus than as the mighty Creator
with power to save or destroy. However, the 'fear of the LORD' is
viewed very positively in the Bible (e.g. Psalm 34:7, 9; Proverbs 1:7;
1 Peter 1:17; Revelation 14:7). Those who truly fear God won't do a
Jonah. But even for hypocrites like him there is a second chance;
read the rest of Jonah and see what happens!

DIG DEEPER!

Can you find the chiasm in Genesis 7:1 – 8:16? Hint:
pay attention to the timings – seven days, forty days,
150 days.

What do we learn about God at the centre of the
chiasm? What is going on at the same time as his
judgment in the flood?

5
The Linking Words Tool

'If', 'since', 'consequently', 'for this reason', 'therefore', 'because', 'so that' – these are all linking words, and they're worth their weight in gold. These words can help us to see the flow of an argument; they reveal cause-and-effect relationships between different statements. As a wise man once said, 'If you see a "therefore", always ask what it's *there for*.' And the same goes for all the other linking words.

'For' and 'therefore'
For and *therefore* are both words that show the flow of thought, but they point in different directions. Because I (Andrew) did a science degree, I find diagrams easier to understand than words, so I like drawing arrows accordingly. (Hey, humour me, OK?)

Therefore arrows go from left from right. What comes before the arrow is the *reason* and whatever comes afterwards is usually the *result* or *consequence* that flows from it. Consider this example:

'I am sending you out like sheep among wolves. $\overrightarrow{Therefore}$ be as shrewd as snakes and as innocent as doves.'
(Matthew 10:16)

Jesus' instruction to be both shrewd and innocent is not just random advice. Such character traits are required of his disciples in the light of the fact that they are being sent into hostile territory. The presence of 'wolves' who will oppose their message is the reason; the need to be shrewd and innocent is the consequence.

Here's another example:

Your attitude should be the same as that of Christ Jesus:

> Who, being in very nature God,
>   did not consider equality with God something
>   to be grasped,
> but made himself nothing,
>   taking the very nature of a servant,
>   being made in human likeness.
> And being found in appearance as a man,
>   he humbled himself
>   and became obedient to death – even death
>   on a cross!
>
> $\overrightarrow{Therefore}$ God exalted him to the highest place
>   and gave him the name that is above every name,
> that at the name of Jesus every knee should bow,
>   in heaven and on earth and under the earth,
> and every tongue confess that Jesus Christ is Lord,
>   to the glory of God the Father.

(Philippians 2:5–11)

This passage is more than a list of the events in Jesus' life – leaving the glory of heaven, becoming a man, dying on a cross, ascending to the highest place. It makes a logical connection between these things. The *reason* God exalted him to the highest place is that he was obedient to die. He humbled himself and *therefore* he was exalted.

For arrows work in exactly the same way, but they point in the opposite direction. This time the reason or explanation comes *after* the arrow:

> Let us hold firmly to the faith we profess. $\overleftarrow{For}$ we do not have a high priest who is unable to sympathise with our weaknesses, but we have one who has been tempted in every way, just as we are – yet was without sin.
> (Hebrews 4:14–15)

You can flip the statement around the other way, and swap the *for* for a *therefore*, and it still means exactly the same thing:

> We do not have a high priest who is unable to sympathise with our weaknesses, but we have one who has been tempted in every way, just as we are – yet was without sin. $\overrightarrow{Therefore}$ let us hold firmly to the faith we profess.

You'll be pleased to know that most other logical linking words behave like these two. After all, there are only two directions in which the arrows can point.

Words like $\overrightarrow{therefore}$	**Words like $\overleftarrow{for}$**
consequently	because
for this reason	since
thus	
so	

If at this stage all these arrows are just confusing you, please ignore them. They help me, but I may just have a quirky mind. The most important thing is not that you draw the arrows, but that you pay attention to what logical connections are being made.

DIG DEEPER!
Read John 7:3–4. At first sight, what do you make of Jesus' brothers' enthusiasm?

There is a linking word in verse 5. In which direction does the argument point? (Draw an arrow if you like.)

What is John telling us about the brothers' PR campaign?

'If' statements

'If you have a nuclear bomb underneath your house, you should drive very fast to somewhere as far away as possible.'

That 'if' statement tells you that a certain action (hurtling down the motorway to nowhere in particular) is recommended in a certain situation (your house is sitting on a block of plutonium). But if your house is OK, then the action isn't such a good idea – in fact, it would be rather a waste of fuel. Thus the advice is *conditional* upon a set of (admittedly rather unfortunate) circumstances.

Here's a biblical example:

> *If* you pay attention to the commands of the LORD your God that I give you this day and carefully follow them, you will always be at the top, never at the bottom ... However, *if* you do not obey the LORD your God and do not carefully follow all his commands and decrees I am giving you today, all these curses will come upon you and overtake you.
> (Deuteronomy 28:13, 15)

These verses lay down an ultimatum for the people of Israel. God's blessing for them is *conditional* upon their keeping the terms of God's covenant. The blessings are not automatic; they can be forfeited *if* the people turn away from their relationship with God. And of course they do turn away, again and again. That's the sad story of the Old Testament. God's people just cannot seem to remain faithful to their God. We see a people desperately in need of rescue and a 'heart transplant' (see Ezekiel 36:26).

However, there is a different kind of biblical *if*, one that doesn't imply uncertainty in the way that our ifs do. When we say, 'If it rains tomorrow, I'll take the train', we imply that it might *not* rain tomorrow. But it doesn't always work like that in Scripture.

> *If* God did not spare angels when they sinned, but sent them to hell, putting them into gloomy dungeons to be held for judgment; *if* he did not spare the ancient world when he brought the flood on its ungodly people, but protected Noah, a preacher of righteousness, and seven others; *if* he condemned the cities of Sodom and Gomorrah by burning them to ashes, and made them an example of what is going to happen to the ungodly; and *if* he rescued Lot, a righteous man, who was distressed by the filthy lives of lawless men (for that righteous man, living among them day after day, was tormented in his righteous soul by the lawless deeds he saw and heard) – *if* this is so, then the Lord knows how to rescue godly men from trials and to hold the unrighteous for the day of judgment, while continuing their punishment.
> (2 Peter 2:4–9)

When Peter says, '*if* [God] condemned the cities of Sodom and Gomorrah', he's not suggesting that there's any doubt about whether it happened. Instead, he's using the *if* to mean something close to an English 'because'. (Try reading it again, substituting the word 'because', and you'll find it makes perfect sense.) Peter's argument goes like this: God has a good track record in sorting out the wicked from the godly – Noah and the flood, Lot trapped in Sodom, etc. And *if* he's done it before (which he *has*, no uncertainty intended), then he knows what to do this time.

'So that'
One final ultra-important linking phrase is 'so that'. Sometimes it is there to tell us the *purpose* behind something:

My dear children, I write this to you so that you will not sin.
(1 John 2:1)

Sometimes it introduces the *result* of something:

Meanwhile, when a crowd of many thousands had gathered,
so that they were trampling on one another.
(Luke 12:1)

You have to use context to decide which it is. In this case it's fairly
obvious that trampling on one another wasn't the *purpose* of the
crowd gathering!

Worked example

Have you ever heard of the Power Team? They're a group of American
weightlifters and musclemen who come over to the UK from time to
time. Here's some of their publicity that I (Andrew) found on the
internet some years ago:

Ripping car license plates, phone books and two decks of cards in
half with their bare hands is no big deal for members of The Power
Team ... These giant men can blow up hot water bottles, snap
baseball bats like twigs, crush through ice with their heads [?!!],
bend steel bars with their teeth ... And they use their muscles for
God. These world-class athletes use phenomenal feats of strength,
power and speed to boldly proclaim the power of Jesus Christ.

The statistics are impressive. According to one article, more than 4,000
people were saved at a five-day crusade in Texas; some 1,700 turned to
Christ at a church in Kansas City.

How does that make you feel? It makes me feel rubbish. Admittedly,
I'm not that envious of the crushing ice with your head thing. But I
wish I could be that successful with my evangelism. I'm not. Far from
being the impressive Christian superstar, when I'm faced with a

confident atheist, I feel very small and unimpressive. I'd never make it on to the spiritual 'Power Team'.

But then neither would the apostle Paul.

In the book of 2 Corinthians, he is defending himself and his ministry in the face of the taunts of some 'super-apostles' who were saying things like this about him: 'His letters are weighty and forceful, but in person he is unimpressive and his speaking amounts to nothing' (2 Corinthians 10:10).

It seems that these super-apostles, by contrast, were great orators, schooled in the Greek art of rhetoric. They were impressive in every way. While Paul spent much of his time banged up in prison, they boasted a more 'successful' type of Christianity. No doubt they had many converts. Probably they charged lots of money for their own spiritual services, and lived in great luxury. It makes you think of some of those modern-day televangelists from the God Channel, who drive around in gold-plated Mercedes and tell you that it's a sign of God's blessing on them – although you can't help thinking that it's got rather more to do with the fact that they keep urging you to dial in with your credit-card details.

Rather surprisingly perhaps, Paul's defence consists of telling the Corinthians just how weak and rubbish he is:

> Five times I received from the Jews the forty lashes minus one.
> Three times I was beaten with rods, once I was stoned, three times
> I was shipwrecked, I spent a night and a day in the open sea . . .
> If I must boast, I will boast of the things that show my weakness.
> (2 Corinthians 11:24–25, 30)

Odd, isn't it? He seems to be playing into his critics' hands. 'Yes, it's true, I am much weaker than them. My version of Christianity is much less impressive than theirs.'

But Paul explains the reason for all this in a series of 'so that' statements that someone armed with the Linking Words tool would never miss:

> We do not want you to be unaware, brothers and sisters, of the
> affliction we experienced in Asia; for we were so utterly, unbearably
> crushed that we despaired of life itself. Indeed, we felt that we had
> received the sentence of death *so that* we would rely not on
> ourselves but on God who raises the dead.
> (2 Corinthians 1:8–9, NRSV)

It is no accident that Paul experiences weakness. It is quite deliberate
on God's part. In his divine sovereignty God arranges things that way *so
that* Paul might trust in God and not in himself:

> We have this treasure in clay jars, *so that* it may be made clear that
> this extraordinary power belongs to God and does not come from us.
> (2 Corinthians 4:7, NRSV)

Clay jars in those days were the equivalent of the disposable plastic
cups that you get in a vending machine. They were worthless. And
Paul is saying that God has chosen to carry the priceless treasure of the
gospel message in containers like that, so that the glory might go to
him alone.

Imagine for a moment that you are a dynamic, witty, good-looking,
brilliant speaker. And through your impressive preaching, someone
becomes a Christian. There would be just no way of knowing, would
there?, whether their conversion was just down to the power of your
sparkling personality.

Imagine instead that you're quite ordinary. Imagine that you tell
someone the gospel with faltering words and a tremor in your voice
because you're so nervous. Imagine that you're unpopular with some
people you know because of your 'extreme' views about religion. And
someone is converted. Well, then, it's obvious, isn't it?, that it's God
who has done it. It's obvious that 'this extraordinary power belongs to
God and does not come from us'.

And so that's the way that God has chosen to work.

DIG DEEPER!

Read Titus chapter 2 in the New International Version. You might want to print out a copy from the internet if you like the idea of drawing arrows all over it.

Highlight all the linking words that you can find.

What is the significance of the *for* that links the two halves of the passage?

How would the thrust of the passage be radically altered if verses 11–14 were not there?

There are three *so thats* in verses 1–10. What is the repeated reason for Christians to live godly lives?

6

The Parallels Tool

Having a toddler has reintroduced me (Nigel) to the nursery rhymes I had largely forgotten. I can now sing 'Twinkle, twinkle little star, how I wonder what you are' all the way through – although I still struggle with the tune.

Now, rhyming 'star' with 'are' isn't great poetry, but it does remind us that *rhyme* is the basic building block of lots of our poetry. However, that isn't the case with the poetry in the Bible. Instead, it uses something called 'parallelism'. Here is an example:

> The earth is the LORD's, and everything in it,
>   the world, and all who live in it;
> for he founded it upon the seas
>   and established it upon the waters.
> (Psalm 24:1–2)

Can you see how the two halves of each verse parallel each other? 'The earth' (line 1) is the same as 'the world' (line 2). 'Founded it upon the seas' (line 3) is equivalent to 'established it upon the waters' (line 4). In both cases, the same thing is said twice in slightly different words. That's the Hebrew way of doing poetry. When you get used to it, you'll find it just as beautiful as a rhyme.

There are a couple of variations on the theme that are worth mentioning briefly. *Antithetical* parallelism is when the second half of the verse gives the opposite perspective to the first half, by way of contrast:

> A fool gives full vent to his anger,
>> but a wise man keeps himself under control.
> (Proverbs 29:11)

Chiastic parallelism is when the second half of the verse says the same as the first half but flips the word order around:

> the torrent would have gone
>> over us;
>> then over us
> would have gone the raging waters.
> (Psalm 124:4–5, NRSV)

In the example above it's particularly effective, because the 'us' is stuck in the middle, swamped by the 'torrent' and the 'raging waters' on either side – and that's exactly what is being described!

Parallelism helps with the meaning

Parallelism is nice because it is poetic, it sounds good. But it can also help us to grasp the *meaning* of a passage. For one thing, it gives you two chances to understand something: if you don't get it the first time, the parallel expression might help.

For example, Isaiah (55:6) urges his hearers to 'Seek the LORD while he may be found.' You might wonder what that means. How do you go about seeking for God? Where are you supposed to look? However, the verse continues: 'call on him while he is near'.

'Seek the LORD' is paralleled by 'call on him'. In other words, we are to seek God by calling out to him in prayer, asking him to help us.

Identifying parallel expressions can help us to unravel obscure verses in other parts of the Bible, even when they're not poetry as such. For example, John's Gospel records these words of Jesus: 'Whoever eats my flesh and drinks my blood has eternal life, and I will raise him up at the last day' (John 6:54). What does it mean to eat Jesus' flesh and drink his blood? Some people might think of Holy Communion, while others think of cannibalism!

However, a few verses earlier Jesus had said this: 'For my Father's will is that everyone who looks to the Son and believes in him shall have eternal life, and I will raise him up at the last day' (John 6:40).

Do you notice how the second half of verse 40 and verse 54 are identical? They parallel each other. That suggests that the first halves of the two verses are also parallel; that is, 'whoever eats my flesh and drinks my blood' parallels 'everyone who looks to the Son and believes in him'.

In other words, the language of eating and drinking Jesus is another way of talking about belief in him. It's a particularly vivid way of saying it, but that's what it means: trusting in his saving death, depending on him for life itself.

Worked example

How would you describe the thrust of the following verse? As comfort or as a challenge?

> If we are faithless, he will remain faithful, for he cannot disown himself.
>
> (2 Timothy 2:13)

You might instinctively interpret it along these lines: even our faithlessness cannot jeopardize our relationship with God, because he is always faithful to us; that is his very nature. That would be a great comfort.

However, it could also be taken another way: beware of turning your back on God. If you do, then in faithfulness to his own character he will turn his back on you. That would be a serious warning.

Both of these options find support elsewhere in the Bible. It's true that God is faithful to forgive us even when we sin (e.g. 1 John 1:9), but it's also true that Jesus promises to reject those who reject him (e.g. Luke 9:26). The question is, which of these is the author's intended meaning, here in 2 Timothy?

Here is the context of the surrounding verses. Can you spot the parallelism?

Here is a trustworthy saying:

> If we died with him,
>   we will also live with him;
> If we endure,
>   we will also reign with him.
> If we disown him,
>   he will also disown us;
> if we are faithless,
>   he will remain faithful,
>   for he cannot disown himself.

(2 Timothy 2:11–13)

Lines 1–2 and 3–4 parallel each other. They are virtually synonymous – if we died/endure, then we will live/reign.

Given that, we would expect lines 5–6 and 7–8 to be parallel, and that is confirmed, as they start in a similar way: to be 'faithless' is the same as to 'disown him'. That parallel suggests that the second halves of the statements are also equivalent – God's remaining faithful is the same as his disowning us.

We are now in a position correctly to interpret the part of the verse that we began with. Far from suggesting that faithlessness on our part doesn't matter, Paul is warning that it has the gravest consequences. If we reject Jesus, he will disown us – because we are rejecting the very source of our salvation and forgiveness.

DIG DEEPER!

In the past God spoke to our forefathers through the prophets at many times and in various ways, but in these last days he has spoken to us by his Son.
(Hebrews 1:1–2)

Can you identify the parallelism in these verses? Is it simple, antithetical or chiastic?

Complete this table, writing in the counterpart to each of the phrases from the first half of the parallelism.

In the past	
God spoke	
to our forefathers	
through the prophets	
at many times and in various ways	

How does the author emphasize that Jesus is the climax of God's revelation to humanity?

Do these verses lead us to expect a further word from God?

7
The Narrator's Comment Tool

Have you ever stood in front of a piece of modern art and wondered what on earth it is all about? It's not particularly complicated – there are only three lines and two blocks of colour on the canvas! But while it's simple at one level, you haven't a clue what is going on.

Imagine that at that moment the artist was standing behind you, and whispered in your ear, 'It's a picture of the disconnectedness of our modern lives.' You look again at the picture, and it makes a bit more sense. There *is* a sense of things being disconnected in the picture. Or maybe, more cheekily, you might feel that the artist is somewhat disconnected from real artistic talent! Perhaps you sense that I (Nigel) am not a great modern-art fan. I admit that most of it goes over my head. But there are times when we have similar feelings when reading parts of the Bible. I'm particularly thinking of narrative passages – we read about people being born, people dying, people becoming kings or slaves, people travelling from one place to another. The events themselves are reasonably straightforward and easy to understand. But what does it mean? So often these stories feel like modern art, where the 'what' is easy (three lines and two blocks of colour), but the 'why' seems beyond reach.

Fortunately, the author occasionally breaks into the narrative and gives us a brief commentary on what is happening, a word of explanation. That's a big help. It is like reading about various events and having the author whisper in our ear, 'This is what is going on!'

Can you spot the narrator's comment in the following verses from Matthew 2?

> When they had gone, an angel of the Lord appeared to Joseph in a dream. 'Get up,' he said, 'take the child and his mother and escape to Egypt. Stay there until I tell you, for Herod is going to search for the child to kill him.'
>
> So he got up, took the child and his mother during the night and left for Egypt, where he stayed until the death of Herod. And so was fulfilled what the Lord had said through the prophet: 'Out of Egypt I called my son.'
> (Matthew 2:13–15)

The last sentence does not tell us anything further about what has happened, about the events themselves. Rather, it gives us Matthew's *explanation* of the events. Matthew tells us that Jesus' being taken to Egypt is more than a matter of saving him from Herod's sword; it also fulfils the promise in the Old Testament (Hosea 11:1) that Jesus would come 'out of Egypt', just as Israel had done during the Exodus. How amazing is God's sovereignty, that even Herod's attempt to kill Jesus leads to the fulfilment of his plan!

What impression do you form of Esau from the following verses?

> Once when Jacob was cooking some stew, Esau came in from the open country, famished. He said to Jacob, 'Quick, let me have some of that red stew! I'm famished!' (That is why he was also called Edom.)

Jacob replied, 'First sell me your birthright.'

'Look, I am about to die,' Esau said. 'What good is the birthright to me?'

But Jacob said, 'Swear to me first.' So he swore an oath to him, selling his birthright to Jacob.

Then Jacob gave Esau some bread and some lentil stew. He ate and drank, and then got up and left.

(Genesis 25:29–34)

From the events alone it's hard to tell. If anything, he comes across as the innocent victim, forced to sell his birthright (the inheritance due to the eldest son) or starve to death. However, the author doesn't leave us to come up with our own interpretation. At this crucial point he supplies a narrator's comment: 'So Esau despised his birthright' (Genesis 25:34).

That casts Esau in a rather different light, doesn't it? All that talk of being 'about to die' was pure exaggeration – he was just hungry, that's all. And his birthright meant so little to him that he was prepared to swap it for a bowl of lentils. When, a couple of chapters later, we find Esau bawling because he's been cut out of his father's will, we aren't quite as sympathetic as we might have been. It serves him right!

Worked example

John chapter 2 describes a visit that Jesus made to the temple in Jerusalem. He was appalled by what he found. Instead of being a place of heartfelt religious devotion, it had become little more than a shopping centre. The various religious service industries – moneychangers, from whom you could obtain the special coins necessary to pay the temple tax; and people selling animals for sacrifices – had moved into the temple courts themselves. You can imagine the cash registers ringing, as the pilgrims were 'processed' as mere commercial traffic. Jesus made a whip and drove out the sheep and cattle; he upturned the tables of the moneychangers, scattering coins everywhere; he spoke in anger to those

present: 'How dare you turn my Father's house into a market.'
Unsurprisingly, the religious authorities got upset:

> Then the Jews demanded of him, 'What miraculous sign can you
> show us to prove your authority to do all this?'
>
> Jesus answered them, 'Destroy this temple, and I will raise it
> again in three days.'
>
> The Jews replied, 'It has taken forty-six years to build this temple,
> and you are going to raise it in three days?' *But the temple he had
> spoken of was his body.* After he was raised from the dead, his
> disciples recalled what he had said. Then they believed the Scripture
> and the words that Jesus had spoken.
>
> (John 2:18–22)

In the Old Testament, the temple was hugely important. It was the
place where God lived among his people and so it was where you went
to meet with God, to offer sacrifices to him or to pray to him. It was
right at the heart of Jewish life and their relationship with God. At the
time of Jesus it had recently been rebuilt and, as we told here, that had
taken forty-six years.

Given all this, Jesus' words seem like nonsense to the people listening
to him. How can he destroy the temple and then raise it in three days?
Indeed, we might have been at a loss to understand it ourselves, were it
not for the narrator's comment (highlighted in italics above). When
Jesus refers to the 'temple' here, he isn't talking about the physical
building they are standing in. He is talking about his own body.

The narrator's comment highlights a huge claim that Jesus is making.
From now on, he is God's temple. He is God's presence on earth, God
dwelling with his people. And consequently he is the place, or rather
the *person*, to whom you must go if you want to meet God.

Actually, this is quite a big theme in John's Gospel. There was a clue
back in chapter 1, where John wrote that 'The Word became flesh and
made his dwelling among us' (John 1:14). A more literal translation

would say that he 'tabernacled' among us, referring to the tabernacle, which was the precursor to the temple. Later, in chapter 4, Jesus says that neither Jerusalem of the Jews nor Mount Gerazim of the Samaritans will be the centre of religious worship in the future. In fact the particular *location* will be irrelevant; what matters is that we worship in spirit and truth, which in the context means worshipping through Jesus.

All this means that to know and worship God, we don't have to go to a special building or special place. The sign on the door of Westminster Abbey that says 'This is the house of God' is wrong! There is no need for the ropes in some churches that keep you out of the most holy bit around the 'altar'. There are no holy places any more, only a holy person. And there should be no altar, because that was something that you had in the temple to make sacrifices for sin, and now Jesus is the temple and he has already made the perfect sacrifice.

Church buildings are useful because they keep the rain off and provide a helpful venue for us to meet with other Christians, which the Bible commands us to do. But you don't need to go to church to meet God – you can do that anywhere, anytime, if you come through Jesus!

DIG DEEPER!

The book of Judges is a prime example of a great story where we can understand what is happening but wonder what it all means.

Read Judges 17:1–6. If you read about the actions of verses 1–5 on their own, what conclusions would you come to?

How does the author's comment in verse 6 help us understand what is going on?

The comment of Judges 17:6 is repeated throughout the book; see 18:1; 19:1; 21:25. What is Israel's big need at this point in her history and why?

The people have their own solution, but it's not the right one. Can you see why, from Judges 8:22–23 and 1 Samuel 8:6–7?

What, or rather who, is God's solution? Read Acts 13:20–23.

8

The Vocabulary Tool

When I (Nigel) was an undergraduate I spent some time studying philosophy. One day I was concentrating hard reading a philosophy textbook, and I have to admit that I was rather pleased that so far I understood what was being said. However, the author then said, ' . . . or to put the matter more simply, the primary epistemological significance of cosmic teleology is . . . ' It didn't really matter what he went on to say. I was lost!

Every field has its own terminology, and it's not uncommon for ordinary words to be invested with a specialist meaning; an 'albatross' means something rather different to a golfer than to a birdwatcher. While technical terms can be intimidating at first sight, we expect you've found that once you spend a little time familiarizing yourself, they're not so hard after all.

The Bible is no different – it too has its own distinctive vocabulary, and uses words in a certain way.

Big Bible words

As you read the Bible you'll come across some words which we use very little in everyday English. They are the Bible's technical terms, what we might call 'big Bible words'. Consider this verse from Paul's letter to the Colossians:

> For he has rescued us from the dominion of darkness and brought us into the kingdom of the Son he loves, in whom we have redemption, the forgiveness of sins.
> (Colossians 1:13–14)

The word 'redemption' comes fairly frequently in the Bible and it has a particular meaning, which it's important that we understand (the same could be said of the word 'kingdom'). The best place to begin is to consult a Bible dictionary. The entry for 'redemption' in 📖 *The New Bible Dictionary* (IVP) tells us: 'Redemption means deliverance from some evil by payment of a price.'

Ultimately words take their meaning from the way that they are used, and so the dictionary entry goes on helpfully to describe the various references to 'redemption' throughout the Old and New Testaments. The archetypal example is God's rescue of Israel from slavery in Egypt. God visited ten horrific plagues on Pharaoh so that he was forced to let Israel go. God then brought Israel through the Red Sea to meet him at Mount Sinai where they were designated his 'treasured possession' (Exodus 19:5). They were bought out of slavery, and now belonged to God. That is redemption.

Having sketched in that background, we can now understand more fully what Paul wrote to the Colossians. Left to ourselves we are all in the dominion of darkness – that is, we are under the power and rule of Satan. But God has acted in Jesus to redeem us and release us from that slavery. Having been rescued, we now belong to God – we have been brought into his kingdom, where he is in charge. You might say that God's rescue of the Israelites from Egypt has been fulfilled in what God has done for us in Jesus.

DIG DEEPER!

> In this is love, not that we have loved God but that he loved us and sent his Son to be the propitiation for our sins.
> (1 John 4:10, ESV)

Look up the word 'propitiation' in a Bible dictionary. Write down a summary of what you learn below.

Propitiation means . . .

Familiar words

We've spoken about words in the Bible that are unfamiliar in modern English. However, words that we use all the time can be even more problematic. We often *assume* we know what they mean without checking whether the Bible is using them in the same way that we do.

For instance, in his letter to Titus, Paul speaks of 'the hope of eternal life' (1:2). We use the word 'hope' a lot today. We hope it won't rain, we hope we'll pass our exams. We use 'hope' to mean something we'd *like* to happen, though we have no certainty that it will happen.

That's not what Paul means by 'hope'. He's talking about something that he is absolutely sure will happen! That becomes clear if we look at the whole verse: 'the hope of eternal life, which God, who does not lie, promised before the beginning of time'. Eternal life has been promised by God. And God doesn't lie. And therefore there is no doubt about this hope. It is certain.

The point is, we must be careful not to assume that the Bible uses a word in the same way as we do.

Words are used in different ways

Sometimes the meaning of a word can vary in the Bible. It might be used differently by different authors, or perhaps by the same author in different contexts.

For example, Jude uses the word 'called' to refer to people who are 'kept by Jesus', that is, Christians:

> To those who have been called, who are loved by God the
> Father and kept by Jesus Christ.
> (Jude 1)

Paul uses it in the same way. He tells of how everyone finds the idea of a crucified Messiah stupid, with the exception of 'those who are called', that is, Christians:

> We preach Christ crucified: a stumbling-block to Jews and
> foolishness to Gentiles, but to those whom God has called,
> both Jews and Greeks, Christ the power of God and the
> wisdom of God.
> (1 Corinthians 1:23–24)

So then, 'called' is almost synonymous with 'Christian'. Since Paul tells us elsewhere that Christians have been chosen by God (e.g. Colossians 3:12; 1 Thessalonians 1:4), we would be right to conclude that all those who are called have been chosen. But what then do you make of these words of Jesus?

> 'For many are called but few are chosen.'
> (Matthew 22:14, ESV)

That statement comes at the end of a parable describing how, out of the many who are invited to a wedding banquet, only a few attend. The 'called' here refers to the large group of people who are invited to know God, many of whom say 'No' to the invitation. In contrast, the 'chosen' are the smaller group of people who accept the invitation and so are saved by Jesus.

Hopefully you can see that the word 'called' is being used in two different ways. Jesus uses it to refer to all those invited to be saved, but for Jude and Paul it refers to those who *are* saved.

If we assumed that 'called' always had the same meaning in the Bible, we would get into trouble with these verses. We would either have to say that everyone who is invited to be saved is saved, which we know isn't true; or we'd have to say that only some of those who are saved are chosen by God, which is equally untrue! Being aware that words can be used differently by different authors will help us avoid such mistakes.

Names

It's worth being aware that biblical names often have special significance. There are some, such as Ichabod, which means 'no glory' (1 Samuel 4:21), or Maher-Shalal-Hash-Baz (*that* would make you wince during school registration), which means 'quick to the plunder, swift to the spoil' (Isaiah 8:1), or even Lo-Ruhamah, which means 'not my loved one' (Hosea 2:23). There are also some glorious ones, such as Samuel, which means 'God heard me', or Jesus, which means 'the LORD saves': 'She will give birth to a son, and you are to give him the name Jesus, because he will save his people from their sins' (Matthew 1:21).

Worked example

The letter we call 'Galatians' was written by Paul to a group of churches in an area of Galatia. Clearly, the group he is writing to includes both men and women. However, in chapter 4 Paul writes that 'because you are *sons* God sent the Spirit of his Son into our hearts, the Spirit who calls out, "Abba Father"' (Galatians 4:6).

Why does Paul say that all Christians, both men and women, are 'sons'? In today's politically correct culture, that sort of thing doesn't go down very well. (Accordingly, some Bible translators change the word 'sons' to 'children'.)

Time to reach for the Vocabulary tool! We need to ask ourselves how Paul is using this word. In particular, does he use it in the same way as we do today, or does it have any special significance? The wider context will help:

> God sent his Son, born of a woman, born under law, to redeem those under law, that we might receive the full rights of sons. Because you are sons, God sent the Spirit of his Son into our hearts, the Spirit who calls out, 'Abba, Father.' So you are no longer a slave, but a son; and since you are a son, God has made you also an heir.
> (Galatians 4:4–6)

There was a great privilege associated with being a son in the ancient world. Paul hints at it when he speaks of the 'full rights' of sons, but then he spells it out – being a son means that you are an *heir*; you stand to inherit all that belongs to your Father.

If you read the rest of Galatians, you'll discover that some people were suggesting that it was necessary to be circumcised in order to receive God's blessings. Paul writes his letter to show that they are wrong. In fact, by trying to add human 'works' to what Jesus has done on the cross, the Galatians were in danger of losing the gospel altogether.

Paul argues that anyone who believes in Jesus is fully accepted by God and so will receive all of God's blessings. All Christians are sons of God!

DIG DEEPER!

Compare these verses, written by Paul and James respectively:

> We maintain that a man is justified by faith apart from observing the law.
> (Romans 3:28)

> You see that a person is justified by what he
> does and not by faith alone.
> (James 2:24)

At first sight we might think Paul and James are contradicting each other. But let's look at the way they use the word 'faith'.

Read Romans 3:28 – 4:8.
How does Paul say someone is 'justified'? And how aren't we justified?

In 4:4–5, how do faith and works function differently?

Sum up what Paul means by 'faith' and 'works' by completing the following sentences:

- Works mean trying to be accepted by God by ...

- Faith means being accepted by God by ...

Using this passage, what would you say to someone who thinks they have to earn their acceptance with God by doing good deeds?

Read James 2:14–24.
Notice that James says in verse 19 that the demons 'believe' ('believe' has the same root as 'faith' in Greek). Now obviously the demons aren't saved, so what does James mean by 'believe' here?

Given that James uses 'faith' to mean merely 'intellectual acknowledgment', why does he say that works are necessary?

Using this passage, what would you say to someone who just intellectually accepts that Jesus died for them, but it doesn't affect their life at all?

Can you now reconcile what Paul and James are saying in these passages? Do you see how they are using the word 'faith' with a different meaning?

9
The Translations Tool

I (Andrew) remember once reading a spoof article in a Christian magazine that poked fun at the massive Christian merchandising industry – fish badges, WWJD bracelets, and so on. At one point, a Christian walks into a multi-storey Christian megastore and asks whether they sell Bibles. 'Oh, yes,' replies the shop assistant, whose teeth are so white when he smiled that the customer must shield his eyes from the sun-reflected glare. 'You want floors eleven through seventeen. Perhaps Madam would be interested in the new Spirit-Filled Housewife's Bible for people who live in houses with thatched roofs? Or maybe you would be more suited to the Working Mother Translation with words of Christ in red, and words of Moses in blue? Or maybe . . . '

Seriously, it does seem that there are endless Bible translations to choose from, and still more come out every year. It's embarrassing, considering that some people in the world still don't yet have any Bible in their language. We would do well to consider making a donation to the Wycliffe Bible Translators before we splash out on another copy in English.

Having said that, there are great advantages in owning more

than one translation, not least because it allows us to use the Translations tool! But first a bit of background.

The Bible was originally written in Hebrew and Greek, Hebrew for the Old Testament (except for a few bits that are in Aramaic) and Greek for the New Testament. Some English versions seek to translate these ancient languages very *literally*, word for word. This means that the reader can get very close to what the Hebrew and Greek are saying, but the disadvantage is that the resulting English can be difficult to read, or even obscure in places.

Take, for example, a literal translation of Genesis 4:1: 'Now Adam knew Eve his wife, and she conceived and bore Cain (English Standard Version). It reads oddly, doesn't it? Obviously Adam *knew* his wife – it would be a strange marriage if they'd never been introduced! But, in fact, to 'know' in Hebrew is a polite way of talking about having sex. That makes much more sense! Adam had sex with Eve and she conceived. But the literal translation retains the exact Hebrew expression and so it's hard to understand.

Other versions have a different translation philosophy. Rather than rendering the Greek and Hebrew word for word, they instead try to translate idea for idea. This is technically known as the principle of 'dynamic equivalence'. The result is a translation that is easier to understand, but not so close to the actual wording of the original. Here is Genesis 4:1 again, this time in a dynamic-equivalent translation: 'Now Adam slept with his wife, Eve, and she became pregnant. When the time came, she gave birth to Cain' (New Living Translation).

Now there's no question that this is easier to understand. But it might lead you into trouble in another way. Suppose you read this verse, and what strikes you is the fact that Cain was born 'when the *time* came' and you make a big point of that: Cain was born at a particular time, the appointed time, perhaps – and your Bible study goes off down that track. The trouble is that the words, 'when the time came' don't appear in the original Hebrew at all. They were just the translator's way of making the sentence flow better in English. Our idea about the 'appointed time' is completely bogus!

The way to avoid gaffes like that is to check what you are reading against more than one than one translation. In particular, if you normally use a dynamic-equivalent translation, we would advise that you buy a literal translation as well.

At the more literal end of the spectrum are the New American Standard Bible (NASB) and the English Standard Version (ESV). The Authorized (King James) Version (AV/KJV) is also literal, but in the few hundred years since it was first published some better Greek manuscripts have come to light and so more recent translations are often to be preferred. At the more 'readable' end the best paraphrase is probably the New Living Translation (NLT). The popular New International Version (NIV) is somewhere in the middle.

Translations and the other tools

One disadvantage of dynamic-equivalent translations is that they can obscure some of the details of the text that we've learnt to value for our toolkit.

Consider this passage from Romans chapter 1:

> I am under obligation both to Greeks and to barbarians, both to the wise and to the foolish. So, for my part, I am eager to preach the gospel to you also who are in Rome. For I am not ashamed of the gospel, for it is the power of God for salvation to everyone who believes, to the Jew first and also to the Greek. For in it the righteousness of God is revealed from faith to faith; as it is written, 'But the righteous man shall live by faith.'
>
> For the wrath of God is revealed from heaven against all ungodliness and unrighteousness of men who suppress the truth in unrighteousness.
> (Romans 1:14–18, NASB)

You could have a field-day with the Linking Words tool here! The backbone of the passage is a whole string of 'For' statements, almost as though Paul keeps anticipating the questions that his readers might be asking:

'I want to preach the gospel also to you who are at Rome.'

'Why so eager, Paul?'

'For I am not ashamed of the gospel.'

'Why not, Paul?'

'For it is the power of God for salvation to everyone who believes.'

'How come, Paul?'

'For in the gospel a righteousness from God is revealed.'

'But why are people in need of being right with God, Paul?'

'For the wrath of God is revealed from heaven . . .'

You can see how crucial the 'Fors' are, in this one big connected argument. But the NIV translators included only two of them. You'd spot the others only if you checked a more literal version like the one above.

Actually, while we're on this, it's worth pausing to think how unfortunate it is to omit the 'For' at the start of verse 18. It might just lead us to miss the connection between our need of salvation and the thing we need saving from, namely God's anger. I think that's happened in a lot of our evangelism. We tell people that they need to be saved, and they are thinking, 'Why? Life is good. I don't need saving any more than someone who is happily tanning themselves on the beach needs to call the coastguard.' And so we try to think of things that Christianity might rescue them from – loneliness maybe, or a sense of lack of fulfilment, or guilt. And that works for a few of our friends who happen to feel lonely or unfulfilled or guilty. But lots of our other friends feel fine, and they remain indifferent and apathetic. But what if we were to explain to them (lovingly) that 'the wrath of God is revealed from heaven' (verse 18) against them, and that in his terrible fury God will one day punish all those who reject his Son and *for that reason* they need to be rescued? People on the beach don't need the coastguard, but when you're drowning in the sea, it's exactly what you need.

Don't get the wrong idea; the NIV is basically a *very good translation*. We don't want you to grow cynical, like some of our non-Christian friends who argue that the Bible is a giant game of

Chinese whispers. It's not! We are privileged to have many excellent Bible translations in the English language. You can trust them. All we're saying is that for *close study* it's good to check more than one, for those relatively few times that it will really matter. A more literal translation is especially good for that.

Worked example

Now Jesus loved Martha, and her sister, and Lazarus. When he had heard *therefore* that he was sick, he abode two days still in the same place where he was.

(John 11:5–6, AV/KJV)

There's an opportunity to use the Linking Words tool if ever there was one! It was *because* Jesus loved Mary and Martha and Lazarus that he delayed in going to Lazarus' sickbed and (if you read on) let him die. But you're thinking, 'That's odd – surely if Jesus loved him he would want to have *stopped* Lazarus from dying?' It seems that the NIV translators thought it was odd too, so they smoothed over it, and softened the 'therefore' into a rather limp 'yet'.

Jesus loved Martha and her sister and Lazarus. Yet when he heard that Lazarus was sick, he stayed where he was two more days.

(John 11:5–6, NIV)

That really is a shame. Although the 'therefore' seems strange, it actually guides us right to the heart of the passage. We're left asking, 'Why was it a loving thing for Jesus deliberately to let Lazarus die? He must have had some greater purpose in Lazarus' death.' And that turns out to be exactly right, as Jesus says explicitly later in the passage (look out for another Linking Word):

So then he told them plainly, 'Lazarus is dead, and for your sake I am glad I was not there, so that you may believe. But let us go to him.'

(John 11:14)

Jesus deliberately let Lazarus die, knowing that he would raise him from the grave. What was his purpose in that? It was *so that* the disciples might believe that he had power over death. It's all very well to believe in heaven 'up there', a kind of ephemeral existence that, if Hollywood is to be believed, resembles an overexposed photograph, since everything is a different shade of white. But Jesus wants us to be confident that the kind of resurrection life that he can give us is a real, *physical*, touch-it-and-see thing. And he wants us to know that fact with a certainty that cannot be shaken even when we are face to face with the dead body of someone we love. So he proves it, in front of eyewitnesses, so that they may believe, and so that we may too, as we read the account of what happened (check out John 20:30–31).

DIG DEEPER!

Read Ephesians 5:18 in the NIV (if you don't have one, you can look on the internet on <http://www.biblegateway.com>). What do you think being 'filled with the Spirit' is about?

How do you know? Where did you get your definition from?

Read Ephesians 5:18–21 in either the ESV or the AV/KJV (more literal translations). Can you see now how verse 18 is connected to what follows?

What four things does Paul associate with being filled with the Holy Spirit?

How does this compare with your definition of a Spirit-filled person?

10
The Tone and Feel Tool

Before you ask, this tool has nothing to do with keep fit!

C. S. Lewis, the Oxford professor who wrote *The Lion, the Witch and the Wardrobe* and other children's stories, used to receive lots of letters from children who admired his books. One budding young writer sent him a story he had written, asking for comments. Lewis wrote back with this advice:

> Instead of telling us a thing is 'terrible', describe it so that we'll be terrified. Don't say 'it was a delight', make us say 'delightful' when we've read the description.[1]

In other words, there is more to language than just conveying statements of fact. Poetry, especially, has the power to change the way we *feel*. Consider this passage from Ezekiel:

> This is what the Sovereign LORD says: Disaster! An unheard-of disaster is coming. The end has come! The end has come!
> It has roused itself against you. It has come! Doom has come upon you – you who dwell in the land. The time has come,

the day is near; there is panic, not joy, upon the mountains.
I am about to pour out my wrath on you and spend my anger
against you . . .

The day is here! It has come! Doom has burst forth, the
rod has budded, arrogance has blossomed! Violence has
grown into a rod to punish wickedness; none of the people
will be left, none of that crowd – no wealth, nothing of value.
The time has come, the day has arrived . . .
(Ezekiel 7:5–12)

If all Ezekiel had wanted to do was to convey a statement of
fact, he could have saved a lot of ink and just written, 'Judgment
day is here.' But somehow that wouldn't have quite the same
effect, would it? Here's a happier example.

Shout for joy to the LORD, all the earth,
    burst into jubilant song with music;
make music to the LORD with the harp,
    with the harp and the sound of singing,
with trumpets and the blast of the ram's horn –
    shout for joy before the LORD, the King.
(Psalm 98:4–6)

Our paper-saving paraphrase: 'Make various musical sounds to
show that you are happy about the LORD.'

A good substitute? No. It means the same, but it's drained of all
the excitement of the original.

The Tone and Feel tool reminds us that as we come to the
Bible, we should pay attention not only to the point that is
being made (although that is the first priority), but also *how* it
is being made. We mustn't reduce the richness of Bible literature
simply to a list of logical statements; we want to be alert to the
author's *tone*, to immerse ourselves in the picture that he paints in
such a way that our imaginations are awakened and our emotions
are engaged. We ought to experience the urgency of 2 Timothy 4,

the anguish of Lamentations 1, the majesty of Job 38, the relief of 2 Samuel 22, the joy of Ephesians 1. It's not very British, perhaps, but it's right to cry sometimes when we read the Bible. And when the Psalms tell us to shout for joy, maybe we should do that too!

Let's think about a couple of different ways this works out in practice. With a narrative, it's often the small details that put flesh on the bones, and make the story more three-dimensional. Perhaps a particular character is brought to the fore, and the writer spends a little extra time sketching their circumstances so that we can really identify with them.

DIG DEEPER!
Look at the four incidents recorded in Mark 4:35 – 5:43. How does Mark's use of detail help us to feel the extent of human helplessness before Jesus steps in?

Read 1 Samuel 1. How does the writer enable us to identify with Hannah's situation so that we are genuinely relieved and delighted when God intervenes?

When it comes to poetry, look out for the use of simile and metaphor, which explain reality by drawing a comparison with something else. Here's an example from the beginning of Psalm 42:

> As the deer pants for streams of water,
>   so my soul pants for you, O God.
> My soul thirsts for God, for the living God.
> (verses 1–2)

The writer wants us to imagine a deer, perhaps on a hot day, perhaps exhausted after fleeing a predator. It is desperately thirsty. It needs to find water as if life depended on it.

That's how this man feels. He is desperate for God. And while God seems so distant, he is on the brink of despair. A series of metaphors conveys his emotional turmoil much more powerfully than would a clinical description:

My tears have been my food day and night.
(verse 3)

Deep calls to deep
    in the roar of your waterfalls;
all your waves and breakers
    have swept over me.
(verse 7)

My bones suffer mortal agony.
(verse 10)

At the other end of the emotional spectrum, Isaiah describes the kind of scene that might be found in a Walt Disney cartoon, as he seeks to convey an overwhelming sense of wonder at the future God has prepared for his people:

You will go out in joy
    and be led forth in peace;
the mountains and hills
    will burst into song before you,
and all the trees of the field
    will clap their hands.
(Isaiah 55:12)

Do you get a sense of the tone and feel of these passages? One way to think about it is to ask what kind of soundtrack would be needed if you were making the film. A slow lament on a single violin, as in *Schindler's List*? A trumpet fanfare? Louis Armstrong singing 'What a wonderful world'?

Worked example

The book of Hosea begins like this:

> When the LORD began to speak through Hosea, the LORD said to
> him, 'Go, take to yourself an adulterous wife and children of
> unfaithfulness . . .
>
> (Hosea 1:2)

It's put very briefly, but when we stop and think about it, it is
horrific. 'Hosea, I want you to marry a whore. Your wife will be
someone who will sleep around and be unfaithful to you.'

It's not hard to imagine Hosea's response: 'But, Lord, why?
I want a wife to love me and be faithful to me! Why put me through
that?'

God's answer is given in the second half of the verse:

> . . . because the land is guilty of the vilest adultery in departing from
> the LORD.
>
> (Hosea 1:2)

God is saying, 'Hosea, I want your marriage to act out my
relationship with my people. I want people to come and look at your
marriage, and wonder, "Hosea, why have you married a harlot, like
that?" And you will reply, "Because that is what you've been like with
God. In your relationship with God you have committed spiritual
adultery." '

Israel was in an exclusive relationship with God. He was their God,
they were his people. They belonged to him. But Hosea goes on to tell
us how the Israelites worshipped other gods. Spiritually speaking, they
had jumped into bed with someone else.

Talk about Tone and Feel! This is one of the most striking
metaphors in the Bible – especially when personally dramatized in
the life of Hosea. It's easy to think of sin merely as breaking some

abstract law, but Hosea shows us that it's much more personal than that. It is unfaithfulness to a divine husband (compare 2 Corinthians 11:1–3).

Thankfully, Hosea doesn't stop there! The metaphor continues a couple of chapters later:

> The LORD said to me, 'Go, show your love to your wife again, though she is loved by another and is an adulteress. Love her as the LORD loves the Israelites, though they turn to other gods and love the sacred raisin cakes.'
> (Hosea 3:1–2)

It seems that Hosea's wife is now in a relationship with another man, but God tells him to take her back. Again it doesn't take much to imagine how Hosea might have felt! You can almost hear him saying, 'But, God! She has hurt me so much. To love her again feels crazy!'

You can imagine the reaction of Hosea's family and friends too: 'Hosea, what are you playing at? To have her back, after all she has done to you – that's unbelievable!'

But once again there's a reason: 'Love her as the LORD loves the Israelites, though they turn to other gods' (Hosea 3:1). In other words, Hosea is to reply to his friends, 'You're right. It is mad, crazy, to love the adulterous. But that is how God feels about you. Despite all your sin, he loves you with a crazy, unbelievable kind of love.'

We mentioned above that we should sometimes cry or shout for joy when we read the Bible. Maybe here we should do both, as we see the amazing love God has for us, despite our terrible spiritual adultery. As the apostle Paul puts it: 'God demonstrates his love for us in this: While we were still sinners, Christ died for us' (Romans 5:8).

DIG DEEPER!

The prophet Jeremiah uses the image of water in many different ways. What sense is being conveyed by the following metaphors? Which one strikes you most forcefully at the moment?

- Jeremiah 2:13, 18

ndon: Geoffrey Bless,

11
The Repetition Tool

One of the ways a Bible writer can get our attention or make sure we don't miss something important is to say it more than once. Ours ears should always prick up if we see the same word or phrase cropping up again and again. It is obviously something the author wanted us to notice – very possibly the heart of what he is saying.

Consider this passage from John 6, in which Jesus explains the significance of the feeding of the 5,000:

> 'I tell you the truth, he who believes has *everlasting life*. I am the bread of *life*. Your forefathers ate the manna in the desert, yet they *died*. But here is the bread that comes down from heaven, which a man may eat and *not die*. I am the *living* bread that came down from heaven. If anyone eats of this bread, he will *live for ever*. This bread is my flesh, which I will give for the *life* of the world.'
>
> Then the Jews began to argue sharply among themselves, 'How can this man give us his flesh to eat?'
>
> Jesus said to them, 'I tell you the truth, unless you eat the flesh of the Son of Man and drink his blood, you have no *life* in

you. Whoever eats my flesh and drinks my blood has *eternal life*, and I will raise him up at the last day. For my flesh is real food and my blood is real drink. Whoever eats my flesh and drinks my blood remains in me, and I in him. Just as the *living* Father sent me and I *live* because of the Father, so the one who feeds on me will *live* because of me. This is the bread that came down from heaven. Your forefathers ate manna and *died*, but he who feeds on this bread will *live for ever*.' He said this while teaching in the synagogue in Capernaum.
(John 6:47–59)

Once we notice the repetition (see italics), the main thrust of the passage is obvious – Jesus is able to give us eternal life! In fact, if you're sharp you will have noticed that something else is repeated, namely the fact that Jesus 'comes/came down from heaven' (three times). Putting it together, we might say that Jesus came down from heaven to give us eternal life. Now that doesn't exhaust the meaning of these verses – there's plenty that the Repetition tool doesn't unlock – but we've made a pretty good start nonetheless.

Another striking example of repetition is found in Daniel chapter 3:

King Nebuchadnezzar made an image of gold, ninety feet high and nine feet wide, and *set it up* on the plain of Dura in the province of Babylon. He then summoned the satraps, prefects, governors, advisers, treasurers, judges, magistrates and all the other provincial officials to come to the dedication of the image he had *set up*. So the satraps, prefects, governors, advisers, treasurers, judges, magistrates and all the other provincial officials assembled for the dedication of the image that King Nebuchadnezzar had *set up*, and they stood before it.
    Then the herald loudly proclaimed, 'This is what you are commanded to do, O peoples, nations and men of every language: As soon as you hear the sound of the horn, flute, zither, lyre, harp, pipes and all kinds of music, you must

fall down and worship the image of gold that King
Nebuchadnezzar has *set up*. Whoever does not fall down and
worship will immediately be thrown into a blazing furnace.'
   Therefore, as soon as they heard the sound of the horn,
flute, zither, lyre, harp and all kinds of music, all the peoples,
nations and men of every language fell down and worshipped
the image of gold that King Nebuchadnezzar had *set up*.
(Daniel 3:1–7)

The writer is poking fun at Nebuchadnezzar's statue. He made
people worship it as though it were a god, but in fact it is only
something he has 'set up' (five times; see italics) – hardly a very con-
vincing deity. But there's even more repetition than that. The writer
also rehearses at length the different ranks in Nebuchadnezzar's
Civil Service – 'the satraps, prefects, governors, advisers, treasurers,
judges, magistrates and all the other provincial officials' (three
times: verses 2, 3, 27) – and he catalogues over and over again the
musical instruments that were played to call people to worship
the golden statue – 'the horn, flute, zither, lyre, harp, pipes and all
kinds of music' (four times: verses 5, 7, 10, 15) – all of which serves to
mock and ridicule the whole pompous affair.
   Coloured pencils or highlighter pens are the friend of the
Repetition tool. Choose a different colour for each repeated
feature that you notice.

Repeated ideas

The repetition tool works not only for repeated words or phrases,
but also for repeated *ideas*. Thus, in chapter 15 of his Gospel, Mark
is keen for us to grasp that Jesus really died – something that
Muslims still deny. So he tells us that Jesus 'breathed his last'
(verse 37, also verse 39 in a literal translation), but also that Pilate
'was surprised to hear that he was already dead' (verse 44); and so
he summoned the centurion to ask 'if Jesus had already died'
(verse 45) and then gave his 'body' (the word means 'corpse') to
Joseph of Arimathea (verse 45) who put it in a 'tomb' (verse 46).

Without repeating many of the same words, Mark has mentioned the same *idea* around six times. It's as if he is saying, 'Jesus died, and, by the way, he died, and did I mention that he died?'

Another example comes in 2 Timothy 2:3–6:

Endure hardship with us like a good soldier of Christ Jesus. No-one serving as a soldier gets involved in civilian affairs – he wants to please his commanding officer. Similarly, if anyone competes as an athlete, he does not receive the victor's crown unless he competes according to the rules. The hardworking farmer should be the first to receive a share of the crops.

At first sight these three pictures of how a gospel worker should behave seem quite different. Soldiers fight, athletes run races, farmers drive tractors ... and a Bible study could very easily start speculating about many and varied connections between living as a Christian and each of these professions. However, a bit of thought reveals that these pictures have something in common: they are all situations where hardship *now* brings reward *later*. The soldier has a tough time on the battlefield, but gets mentioned in dispatches when he returns; the athlete trains hard for months, but eventually wins a trophy; the farmer sows and ploughs and waters, but then finally he has a harvest. Suffering now, glory later.

If we read on in 2 Timothy 2 we find that the same point is made by Jesus' example (verse 8) and Paul's example (verses 9–10), and then it comes twice in Paul's trustworthy saying (verses 11–12). Every time, it is in different words, but the *idea* is repeated again and again. The whole is greater than the sum of the parts, they say, and here it is true. It is the common theme we should focus on, and it is a vital and wonderful lesson to learn: we will suffer now, but it's worth it!

Repetition and the other tools

So far, this tool sounds pretty good. All you have to do is find something that the author says more than once, put it in the slot, turn the handle, and out comes the main point of the passage. Hmm. Sadly, it's not quite as simple as that. Consider this example from the book of Revelation:

> 'When the kings of the earth who committed adultery with her and shared her luxury see the smoke of her burning, they will weep and mourn over her. Terrified at her torment, they will stand far off and cry:
>
> > ' "Woe! Woe, O great city,
> >   O Babylon, city of power!
> > In one hour your doom has come!"
>
> 'The merchants of the earth ... will stand far off, terrified at her torment. They will weep and mourn and cry out:
>
> > ' "Woe! Woe, O great city,
> >   dressed in fine linen, purple and scarlet,
> >   and glittering with gold, precious stones and pearls!
> > In one hour such great wealth has been brought to ruin!"
>
> 'Every sea captain, and all who travel by ship, the sailors, and all who earn their living from the sea, will stand far off. When they see the smoke of her burning, they will exclaim, "Was there ever a city like this great city?" They will throw dust on their heads, and with weeping and mourning cry out:
>
> > ' "Woe! Woe, O great city,
> >   where all who had ships on the sea
> >   became rich through her wealth!
> > In one hour she has been brought to ruin!'
> > Rejoice over her, O heaven!
> >   Rejoice, saints and apostles and prophets!
> > God has judged her for the way she treated you." '
>
> (Revelation 18:9–11, 15–20)

The important point here is not the distance of the ungodly from Babylon ('far off'), or the exact wording of their cry ('Woe! Woe, O great city'), or even the time taken for the profits of godless materialism to be destroyed ('one hour'), even though each of these features is repeated in the text. In fact, the most important theological statement is made only once, in the last sentence. Rather than highlighting a particular truth, the purpose of the repetition here is to set a set a certain tone. This is a lament. People are wringing their hands, shaking their heads, crying out over and over. We're supposed to feel that; it's supposed to capture our imaginations. Why envy the ungodly for their prosperity, when it will all end in tears? Who would want to be one of them? You might say that this is a case of Repetition tool meets Tone and Feel tool.

On other occasions, repetition might prompt us to reach for our Structure tool. We have already seen how the repetition of 'voice' in Isaiah 40, or the 'next day' in John 1, helps us to break those passages down into paragraphs. In Genesis we find that each major section is introduced by the repeated phrase 'this is the account of . . .' (see 2:4; 5:1; 6:9; 10:1; 11:10; 11:27; 25:12; 25:19; 36:1; 37:2).

If you want to have a go, other particularly good places to practise using the Repetition tool include Genesis chapter 1 and Exodus chapters 8 – 11.

Worked example

You probably know these famous verses from Isaiah:

> Surely he took up our infirmities
>   and carried our sorrows,
> yet we considered him stricken by God,
>   smitten by him, and afflicted.
> But he was pierced for our transgressions,
>   he was crushed for our iniquities;

the punishment that brought us peace was upon him,
  and by his wounds we are healed.
We all, like sheep, have gone astray,
  each of us has turned to his own way;
and the LORD has laid on him the iniquity of us all.
(Isaiah 53:4–6)

The New Testament makes clear that this prophecy, written in the eighth century BC, finds it fulfilment in the death of Jesus on the cross (1 Peter 2:22–25; Acts 8:26–35). But what is the main idea that we are to take away from it? Are we to put the emphasis on the similarities between humans and sheep – always prone to wandering off? Or should we highlight the physical suffering that Jesus endured on the cross as he was 'crushed' and 'afflicted'? Those ideas are certainly present in the passage. But the central point is made again and again by the pairs of repeated pronouns, 'he', 'our', 'him', 'us', and the constant swapping between them. That shows us that Jesus died as a substitute. It was a case of him instead of us. He took on himself the punishment due to us, because of our 'transgressions' and 'iniquity', so that we could go free.

Charles Dickens' *A Tale of Two Cities* is set during the French Revolution. Two of the central characters are Charles Darnay, a French aristocrat, and Sydney Carton, an English lawyer. As it happens, they look strikingly similar. They both love the same woman, Lucie Manette, but it's Darnay who wins her. Towards the end of the book Darnay goes to France – not a good move for an aristocrat during the revolution – and sure enough he ends up in prison facing the guillotine.

The night before he is executed, Carton goes with a helper to the prison to visit him. He shows his papers at the gate, 'Sydney Carton, Englishman', and is let in. Once in his cell Carton gives Darnay a drink that contains a sedative. He then changes clothes and papers with Darnay. The helper carries out the sleeping Darnay to the carriage, then goes to the gate, announces 'Sydney Carton, Englishman', and he is let out to freedom. Meanwhile the real Carton is back in the cell, and the next day he is led out and executed.

That is what Jesus has done for us. We are guilty and face death and God's judgment. But Jesus, the innocent, is punished on our behalf, that we might go free. It is the most extraordinary swap in the world!

DIG DEEPER!

Read Daniel 4. An important statement about God occurs three times (and then it comes again in chapter 5). Can you spot it?

How does this recurring slogan help to unlock the meaning of the chapter?

When Nebuchadnezzar invaded Jerusalem, desecrated the temple and took God's people into exile (read 2 Kings 25 for more details), it must have looked as though he was more powerful than the LORD. How does Daniel 4 answer that fear?

How might our repeated phrase comfort those Christians in today's world who are suffering under political regimes that are hostile to their faith? Who is pulling the strings behind the superpowers of our own day, both the ones we like and the tyrannical ones that we don't?

12

The Quotation/Allusion Tool

Throughout this book we've tried to quote passages from the Bible to explain and back up what we're saying. Sometimes we quote only a few words, and you might want to go back and read the whole paragraph or chapter to get the context.

Sometimes the Bible quotes the Bible too. Later writers (e.g. Paul) may quote earlier writers (e.g. Moses) to explain and back up what they're saying. Sometimes they quote only a few words, and you might want to go back and read the whole paragraph or chapter to get the context.

In fact, it's always a good idea to *look up the original context of a quotation*, in case the later writer wants to us to think not just about the few words that he copies out, but the whole of the section that they were taken from. Many modern Bibles will give you the appropriate cross-reference in a footnote.

Here's an example:

He [Jesus] went to Nazareth, where he had been brought up, and on the Sabbath day he went into the synagogue, as was his custom. And he stood up to read. The scroll of the prophet Isaiah was handed to him. Unrolling it, he found the place where it is written:

> 'The Spirit of the Lord is on me,
>> because he has anointed me
>> to preach good news to the poor.
> He has sent me to proclaim freedom for the prisoners
>> and recovery of sight for the blind,
> to release the oppressed,
>> to proclaim the year of the Lord's favour.'

Then he rolled up the scroll, gave it back to the attendant and sat down. The eyes of everyone in the synagogue were fastened on him, and he began by saying to them, 'Today this scripture is fulfilled in your hearing.'
(Luke 4:16–21)

As Jesus quotes from Isaiah 61, he does two extraordinary things. The first is that he applies the prophecy to himself, tantamount to saying, 'I am the Messiah', which must have astounded the first hearers. The second is that he ends the quotation in mid-sentence. You'd only know that if you looked up the original context. Here it is:

> The Spirit of the Sovereign LORD is on me,
>> because the LORD has anointed me
>> to preach good news to the poor.
> He has sent me to bind up the broken-hearted,
>> to proclaim freedom for the captives
>> and release from darkness for the prisoners,
> to proclaim the year of the LORD's favour
>> and the day of vengeance of our God.
> (Isaiah 61:1–2)

In Isaiah, the year of God's favour and the day of his judgment come together (see also Isaiah 63:4). But by cutting off the quotation halfway through, Jesus seems to be saying in effect, 'This is the year of God's favour. It's come. But it isn't yet the day of judgment!'

That doesn't mean that Jesus doesn't believe in judgment day; some of his other teaching is pretty explicit about that. It just means that God's favour has come early, if you like, in advance of his judgment. There's time to repent and believe and receive forgiveness before the 'day' comes.

Here's another example, from John's account of the crucifixion:

Now it was the day of Preparation, and the next day was to be a special Sabbath. Because the Jews did not want the bodies left on the crosses during the Sabbath, they asked Pilate to have the legs broken and the bodies taken down. The soldiers therefore came and broke the legs of the first man who had been crucified with Jesus, and then those of the other. But when they came to Jesus and found that he was already dead, they did not break his legs. Instead, one of the soldiers pierced Jesus' side with a spear, bringing a sudden flow of blood and water. The man who saw it has given testimony, and his testimony is true. He knows that he tells the truth, and he testifies so that you also may believe. These things happened so that the scripture would be fulfilled: 'Not one of his bones will be broken,' and, as another scripture says, 'They will look on the one they have pierced.' (John 19:31–37)

What is the significance of those quotations? The first comes from Exodus 12:46, talking about the Passover sacrifice. You will remember that God told the Israelites to sacrifice a lamb and to smear its blood on their doorposts. Then, as the Destroyer passed through the land, when he saw the blood on the door, he 'passed over' that house and spared the firstborn son. God's judgment was averted by a sacrifice, the substitutionary death of an animal. What you might not have known is that the Israelites were specifically instructed not to break the bones of the Passover lamb, a detail later replicated in the death of Jesus. Jesus fulfils the Passover. His death is the true sacrifice that saves his people from God's judgment.

The second quotation comes from Zechariah 12:10, speaking of a day when 'they will look on me, the one they have pierced'. Again the context is instructive, for if we read on, a few verses later, we discover that on that same day, 'a fountain will be opened to the house of David and the inhabitants of Jerusalem, to cleanse them from sin and impurity' (Zechariah 13:1).

John is using Zechariah to tell us that, on the day that Jesus is pierced and dies, it as though a fountain is opened to wash us clean of all our sin and wrongdoing. Wow!

Allusions

Allusions are harder to spot than quotations, because there's nothing explicit to tell you that another part of the Bible is being referred to – no 'it is written' or 'this happened to fulfil the words of the prophet' or anything like that. Just an echo of another part of Scripture, which you'll notice only if you're tuned in.

If I told you that yesterday, all my troubles seemed so far away, you would immediately recognize an allusion to a famous song by the Beatles. How about if you heard the start of this parable?

A man planted a vineyard. He put a wall around it, dug a pit for the winepress and built a watchtower. Then he rented the vineyard to some farmers and went away on a journey.
(Mark 12:1)

If you were a first-century Jew, you would immediately think, 'Ah, yes, he's picking up the language of Isaiah chapter 5!' Similarly, when Jesus' contemporaries heard his description of the kingdom of heaven as a huge tree with the birds of the air perching in its branches (Matthew 13:32), they would pick up the echo of Ezekiel 31 and Daniel 4, which had described the earthly superpowers of Assyria and Babylon in those same terms.

Of course, our problem is that we don't know the Old Testament well enough to spot these allusions. A cross-reference Bible will often get you off the hook, but you shouldn't miss the challenge of getting to know the Bible better for yourself! One way to do that would be to get hold of a copy of the McCheyne Bible Reading Calendar (The International Fellowship of Evangelical Students publishes it in a little leaflet called *More Precious than Gold*, or you can download it from the internet at <http://hippocampusextensions.com/mcheyneplan.html>). This takes you through the Old Testament once and the New Testament twice each year. It takes me about fifteen minutes morning and evening to read through the four chapters prescribed for each day. It's amazing how quickly you begin to spot connections between different things you read.

Use of the same word or idea by two biblical authors does not *necessarily* imply a connection. So, for instance, the fact that Jesus rode into Jerusalem on a donkey (John 12:14) is entirely unrelated to Samson having killed a thousand men with the jawbone of a donkey (Judges 15:15–16) or Saul having been looking for lost donkeys when he first met the prophet of God (1 Samuel 9). Donkeys were fairly common things in those days, that's all. Jesus riding on a donkey *is* related to the prophecy in Zechariah 9:9 about donkeys, but we know that only because John quotes it explicitly.

So how can you tell if an allusion is real or spurious? A general rule of thumb is that the more specific or unusual the expression, the less likely it is that its use in two places in the Bible is coincidental. If sheep are mentioned in two places, it's no big deal. But the phrase 'sheep without a shepherd' is distinctive enough that when it comes up in both Mark 6:34 and Numbers 27:17 it can hardly be an accident.

The covenant with Abraham

God's promise or 'covenant' with Abraham is alluded to so often that it merits special mention. Beginning in Genesis 12, God promises Abraham three things, namely:

- many descendants (e.g. Genesis 13:16; 15:5)
- a land for them to live in (e.g. Genesis 12:7; 13:14–15)
- God's blessing on them and others through them
  (e.g. Genesis 12:2–3)

This promise is then repeated to Abraham's son, Isaac:

'Stay in this land for a while, and I will be with you and will bless you. For to you and your descendants I will give all these lands and will confirm the oath I swore to your father Abraham. I will make your descendants as numerous as the stars in the sky and will give them all these lands, and through your offspring all nations on earth will be blessed.'
(Genesis 26:3–4)

and to his grandson, Jacob:

There above it stood the LORD, and he said: 'I am the LORD, the God of your father Abraham and the God of Isaac. I will give you and your descendants the land on which you are lying. Your descendants will be like the dust of the earth, and you will spread out to the west and to the east, to the north and to the south. All peoples on earth will be blessed through you and your offspring.'
(Genesis 28:13–14)

These promises are absolutely foundational for the rest of the Old Testament, even the whole of the Bible, as they spell out God's great plan for a restored humanity. It's no wonder, then, that there are many allusions to them throughout the Bible. Here are some examples:

God heard their groaning and he remembered his covenant with Abraham, with Isaac and with Jacob.
(Exodus 2:24)

'Remember your servants Abraham, Isaac and Jacob.
Overlook the stubbornness of this people, their wickedness
and their sin.'
(Deuteronomy 9:27)

David did not take the number of the men twenty years old
or less, because the LORD had promised to make Israel as
numerous as the stars in the sky.
(1 Chronicles 27:23)

If you belong to Christ, then you are Abraham's seed, and
heirs according to the promise.
(Galatians 3:29)

Quotations or allusions like this help us understand what is
happening in the passage we are reading; in the cases above it is
that God is fulfilling his great promise to Abraham. In fact, seeing
this promise being fulfilled throughout the Bible teaches us a great
truth about God: he is faithful and always keeps his promises. That
is a great encouragement to us always to trust and obey what
he says.

Worked example

The book of Ezra describes a time near the end of Old Testament
history, when the Israelites returned from exile in Babylon to rebuild
the fallen city of Jerusalem. Among other things, it describes
paradoxically different responses to the laying of the temple
foundation:

When the builders laid the foundation of the temple of the LORD,
the priests in their vestments and with trumpets, and the Levites
(the sons of Asaph) with cymbals, took their places to praise the
LORD, as prescribed by David king of Israel. With praise and
thanksgiving they sang to the LORD:

'He is good;
    his love to Israel endures for ever.'

And all the people gave a great shout of praise to the LORD, because
the foundation of the house of the LORD was laid. But many of the
older priests and Levites and family heads, who had seen the former
temple, wept aloud when they saw the foundation of this temple
being laid, while many others shouted for joy. No-one could
distinguish the sound of the shouts of joy from the sound of
weeping, because the people made so much noise. And the sound
was heard far away.
(Ezra 3:10–13)

Why are the senior citizens so miserable? There's a clue in the fact
that they had 'seen the former temple'. Perhaps they recognize
something tragically deficient about this one by comparison?

Our Quotation/Allusion tool can help us here. The mention of
trumpets and cymbals and the words of the song, 'He is good; his
love ... endures for ever', are an unmistakable allusion to 2 Chronicles
5:13–14, the description of the dedication of the first temple. But there is
a key difference.

The trumpeters and singers joined in unison, as with one voice,
to give praise and thanks to the LORD. Accompanied by trumpets,
cymbals and other instruments, they raised their voices in praise to
the LORD and sang:

'He is good;
    his love endures for ever.'

Then the temple of the LORD was filled with a cloud, and the priests
could not perform their service because of the cloud, for the glory of
the LORD filled the temple of God.

Did you spot the difference? In Ezra there is no glory. No cloud of God's presence descends. No wonder there is weeping. A temple without God's glory in it is a mere shell.

While in Ezra's day it was right for the Israelites to build the temple, this allusion to 2 Chronicles makes us look and long for the time God's temple will be fully restored – the day his glory comes to it. That is the note on which the Old Testament closes, pointing us forward to a future day – the day the glory did come to God's temple. Not in a cloud, but in the person of a Nazarene carpenter, of whom John wrote: 'We have seen his glory, the glory of the One and Only, who came from the Father, full of grace and truth' (John 1:14).

DIG DEEPER!

In the Garden of Gethsemane, Jesus refers metaphorically to a 'cup' of which he seems to be afraid (Mark 14:36). That's not much to go on, because like donkeys in the example above, cups are quite common things. Nonetheless, there are a couple of dominant Old Testament metaphors to which Jesus might have been alluding. From the context in Mark, which of these sets of passages is the better fit? Please look them all up, even if you get the general idea, so you get the full impact.

Psalm 16:15; 23:5

Psalm 75:8; Isaiah 51:17; Jeremiah 25:15–16; Lamentations 4:21; Ezekiel 23:31–34; Habakkuk 2:16

Can you explain why *Jesus* should find himself drinking this cup, given the one for whom it was originally intended in the passages cited?

13
The Genre Tool

You might be familiar with the concept of 'genre' from film reviews – horror movie, western, black comedy, chick flick, documentary – those are all *genres*. It's a way of classifying media according to their type or style rather than their specific content or storyline. There are many different genres in the Bible – songs, prophecies, proverbs, laments, visions, speeches, parables, historical narrative. Identifying the genre is very important to how we interpret a passage.

When David says in Psalm 22, 'I am poured out like water', he is not describing a miracle in which his whole body became a liquid. It's poetry; we're not supposed to take it literally. On the other hand, when the Gospels record that the tomb was empty, they mean that it physically was. The resurrection of Jesus is not a metaphor.

Sadly, we can't give you a guaranteed 100%-accurate way of deciding on the genre of a passage. Occasionally it is controversial, such as with Genesis chapter 1, where there has been much debate on whether the creation in six 'days' refers to a literal period of 6 × 24 hours, or whether it is a poetic way of speaking about the careful, ordered way in which God made the universe. Most of the time, however, it is fairly obvious.

Once you've decided on the genre, here are two general principles to follow:

1. When something is presented as historical fact, pause to consider that it really happened.
2. When something is presented as imagery/metaphor, don't base crazy predictions of the future on its being literally and physically true.

Stuff that really happened

When we say you should pause to consider that historical things really happened, we're talking about the danger of jumping so quickly to the spiritual lesson behind an event that we miss the fact that it was an *event* at all.

Take, for example, the crossing of the Red Sea in Exodus 14. It has great theological significance as the Old Testament example *par excellence* of God's deliverance; there are loads of cross-references we could look at with regard to its deeper spiritual meaning. But before we do any of that we ought to stop for a moment and think: 'Hang on a minute, this actually occurred! God parted the waters of the sea, and made the water on each side stand up like a wall. And the people walked through the middle, and it was *dry*! If time travel were possible, and you set the dial to 1447 BC or thereabouts, you would be able to see with your own eyes a bunch of people walking through a corridor of air cut through the sea. And then you would see their enemies chasing them with chariots and the walls of water on both sides suddenly crashing down to fill the gap, drowning them in their pursuit. You would actually see that, because this is real history. And that thought should make your heart beat a little faster and sing for joy along with Moses and the Israelites:

'Who among the gods is like you, O LORD?

Who is like you –
majestic in holiness,
awesome in glory,
working wonders?'
(Exodus 15:11)

You may have heard the joke about the liberal theology professor who chose this chapter for a preaching engagement at an Afro-Caribbean church. He had hardly read the first line of the story when he was interrupted by a cry from the back: 'Hallelujah, praise the Lord, that he should part the waters of the mighty Red Sea!' Others joined in with loud Amens and shouts of 'Preach it, brother, preach it!' and outbreaks of applause. He read another line, and the same happened – more Hallelujahs and clapping and shouts of 'I believe it!'

It wasn't long before the professor became a little irritated by these interruptions, not least because they displayed what was, for him, a hopelessly naïve faith in the miraculous. 'Of course, scholars now know', he said rather sniffily, 'that the sea that Moses crossed wasn't the Red Sea at all – it was probably just a swamp a few inches deep.'

But, much to his consternation, the cry went up even louder, 'Hallelujah, praise the Lord ... that he should drown a whole army of Egyptians in a few inches of water!'

Of course, the fact that something happened doesn't mean that it can't have theological or metaphorical significance as well. Miracles, especially, are almost always performed to teach us something; the apostle John prefers to call them 'signs' because, like signposts, they point to a truth beyond themselves. If you did the 'Dig deeper' exercise on Mark 8 (see p. 41), you'll have seen that the healing of the blind man was a metaphor for something else. Fair enough. But there was nonetheless a *historical* blind man who experienced a miraculous change in his retina, optic nerve or visual cortex so that he could see. Let's never forget that the Gospels are not merely a written philosophy but eyewitness testimony to someone whom the apostles had 'seen with our eyes, which we have looked at and our hands have touched' (1 John 1:1).

Stuff that we shouldn't take literally

There are other genres where we need to read things figuratively and not literally. Take parables, for example. The parable of the Sower (Mark 4:1–20) is of rather limited benefit if Jesus is offering agricultural advice. After all, modern farmers have seed drills and combine harvesters. No, the seed in the parable is a metaphor for the message of the gospel (verse 14), and the different 'soils' represent different hearers of the word and how they respond.

We're normally pretty good at switching into non-literal mode when we read parables or poems. Where we sometimes get it wrong is with the genre known as 'apocalyptic' that covers Revelation, Daniel and parts of Ezekiel and Zechariah. Those books are partly made up of visions and dreams and, as such, they contain vivid and sometimes bizarre images, just like our dreams do. If you've come across the popular 'Left Behind' books, you'll know that some Christians take these passages very literally. We think that's a mistake, and we'll try and show you why.

In Revelation 21:2, John sees the heavenly city 'coming down out of heaven'. It isn't that John happened to catch it while it was still moving, before it comes to a stop. When he looks again a few verses later, it is still 'coming down from heaven' (21:10). And according to 3:12, this is what it always does. You're thinking, if it's been coming down for that long, surely it's got to reach its destination some time soon? But that's not the point. This isn't a literal description of movement, but a poetical description of what kind of city it is – a coming-down-from-heaven city! A city that is from God! Notice also that it is the *city* (rather than the inhabitants) that is dressed like a bride (21:2). Skyscrapers wearing wedding dresses sound like something out of a surrealist Salvador Dali picture! Of course, that won't happen *physically*. It's symbolic of the fact that the whole church (the city) is destined for an intimate, permanent, loving relationship with the Lord Jesus Christ, which John likens to a marriage (compare 19:7–9).

A guy called John Richardson, who has written a highly recommended little book on Revelation (📖 *Revelation Unwrapped*, MPA Books), has summed up what we're trying to say with the slogan 'Vision not Video'. Or if you prefer, 'Imagery not IMAX', 'Dream not Documentary', 'Figurative not Fujifilm' – you get the idea!

Just to clinch the point, let's ask the question: how many people will be in heaven? The number given in 7:4 is 144,000, but is that something we should take literally? The Jehovah's Witnesses teach that it is, which apparently caused some problems when the number of JWs worldwide first topped 144,000. That interpretation also runs into difficulty five verses later when John says that the number was so large that 'no-one could count' them. But hang on, I thought he just did? I thought he counted and there were exactly 144,000? No, it's a *symbolic* number. There were twelve tribes in Israel, the people of God (they're listed in the next verse, so we're on the right track), and 12×12 is 144, and 1,000 is just a really big number, so that 144,000 = all Israel $\times$ all Israel $\times$ a whole lot, that is, a breathtakingly huge number of people from every tribe and language and people and nation, whom God will save through the Lord Jesus. We are supposed to be excited by that, but we're not supposed to be keeping tally.

This doesn't mean, by the way, that you're allowed to do loony maths to find hidden symbolism in *all* biblical numbers. In an idle moment, I (Andrew) once calculated that if you take 153 (the number of fish caught by Jesus' disciples in John 21:11) and add 13 (which is supposed to be unlucky) and then add $\frac{1}{2}$ and double it and double it again, you get the number of the beast, 666.

That isn't significant, incidentally. So long as you add the right number, and multiply it by the right thing, then you can get 666 as the outcome of *any* calculation. For example, did you know that 123 (the number of returning exiles from Bethel and Ai, according to Nehemiah 7:32) $\times$ 3 (the number of Persons in the Trinity) + 150 (the number of Psalms) + 147 (maximum break in snooker) is . . . you've guessed it, 666 again. We're choosing deliberately ridiculous examples, but we trust that you won't fall for the ones that get published in bestselling books either.

DIG DEEPER!
Have a go at identifying the genre of the following passages. Should you interpret them as historical or figurative?

Judges 9:8–15

2 Samuel 12:1–6

1 Kings 17:8–16

Ezekiel 46:19–24 (harder – read on into chapter 47)

Matthew 5:29–30

Matthew 14:6–11

Exodus 9:22–24; Revelation 16:21 (You may not get the same answer for both!)

14
The Copycat Tool

When I (Nigel) was learning to drive I can remember watching other people at the wheel and copying what they did. However, many experienced drivers don't drive as you are meant to 'in the test', and so it wasn't long before I was told by those teaching me, 'Drive as I say, not as I do!'

Sometimes we are to follow the example of people we read about in the Bible. But not always! Here are three events in the Bible followed by an interpretation that takes them as an example for us today.

- In Daniel 6, an order is given that prayers may not be offered to anyone but the king of Babylon. Daniel ignores the king's edict and continues to pray to the true God. This means we should copy Daniel and obey God rather than men.
- In 1 Samuel 3 the young boy Samuel hears his name called during the night and thinks it is Eli calling him. Eli tells him it is God speaking to him, which leads to God giving Samuel a prophecy. This means we should expect God to speak to us audibly and tell us what will happen in the future.

- In 2 Samuel 11 King David commits adultery with Bathsheba. This means we too can commit adultery.

What do you think of each of these? I imagine we'd all accept the first one happily. The second we may be more ambivalent about, depending on what we've been taught regarding how God speaks to us today. But I hope we would all disagree with the third! However, all three have 'used' the Bible in the same way.

The point is, we need to be very careful with this 'copycat' approach. Not everything done by a Bible character is good. And even good things they do are not always normative; that is, they may not hold for all Christians at all times.

To put this another way, there is a danger in mistaking something that the Bible *describes* for something that it *prescribes*. The Bible describes what happened to Samuel, as God spoke to him in an audible voice. But just because something happened in a particular way to particular person, it doesn't mean it will happen like that for us all. It isn't necessarily something that is prescribed for us.

Having said that much, we must also be clear that the copycat approach isn't *always* wrong. Sometimes the Bible does hold up people and their various experiences as examples for us to imitate (or avoid):

Brothers, as an example of patience in the face of suffering, take the prophets who spoke in the name of the Lord. (James 5:10)

Join with others in following my example, brothers, and take note of those who live according to the pattern we gave you. (Philippians 3:17)

Now these things occurred as examples to keep us from setting our hearts on evil things as they did. (1 Corinthians 10:6)

How can we know whether any given passage in the Bible is prescriptive or merely descriptive? How can we tell whether or not we should follow someone as an example?

For one thing, we can ask whether it fits with or contradicts what is said elsewhere in the Bible. We would not conclude that adultery is acceptable from our example above, because other parts of Scripture clearly teach otherwise. The better we know our Bibles, the better we will be guarded from drawing wrong conclusions from what we read.

Perhaps the biggest help, though, is the Author's Purpose tool. Does the author *intend* this description to be taken as a prescription for us?

In Judges 6, for example, God instructs Gideon to fight against his enemies, the Midianites and Amalekites, promising their defeat. However, Gideon asks for confirmation:

Gideon said to God, 'If you will save Israel by my hand as you have promised – look, I will place a wool fleece on the threshing-floor. If there is dew only on the fleece and all the ground is dry, then I will know that you will save Israel by my hand, as you said.' And that is what happened. Gideon rose early the next day; he squeezed the fleece and wrung out the dew – a bowlful of water.

Then Gideon said to God, 'Do not be angry with me. Let me make just one more request. Allow me one more test with the fleece. This time make the fleece dry and the ground covered with dew.' That night God did so. Only the fleece was dry; all the ground was covered with dew.
(Judges 6:36–40)

Some Christians have taken this as an example for us to follow, whenever we are need of guidance from God. You may have heard the expression, 'laying a fleece', meaning that we ask God to make a very particular thing happen to indicate what course of action we should take.

However, we should be cautious about this. After all, Gideon wasn't trying to discover what God wanted him to do; God had spoken to him clearly and promised that he would defeat these armies. Rather than guidance, the issue for Gideon is one of assurance – he's scared and wants some encouragement that God will do what he's promised. Gideon's request about the fleece actually comes from his doubt and struggle to obey what God has said.

Given that, it's very unlikely that Gideon is being given to us as an example to follow – and the author certainly gives us no indication of that whatsoever. What it does show us is that God is very patient with those who have weak faith. That is something we should all find encouraging!

We'll look at some different aspects of this issue using the 'Who Am I?' tool and the Bible Timeline tool below. The overall point for now is that we must be careful before we turn a description into a prescription.

This tool is particularly important when we come to the book of Acts, so let's look at two examples from that book.

Worked example 1

Acts contains some wonderful descriptions of the generosity of the first Christians. In particular, we are told about a man named Barnabas:

> All the believers were one in heart and mind. No-one claimed that any of his possessions was his own, but they shared everything they had. With great power the apostles continued to testify to the resurrection of the Lord Jesus, and much grace was upon them all. There were no needy persons among them. For from time to time those who owned lands or houses sold them, brought the money from the sales and put it at the apostles' feet, and it was distributed to anyone as he had need.

> Joseph, a Levite from Cyprus, whom the apostles called Barnabas (which means Son of Encouragement), sold a field he owned and brought the money and put it at the apostles' feet.
> (Acts 4:32–37)

Now, should we take Barnabas as an example to follow? Or, to put it another way, does Luke intend this description to be prescriptive? Note the following points:

1. Luke uses repetition to emphasize the lesson of generosity. The generosity of the church is highlighted not only in the passage quoted above, but also in Acts 2:44–45. Luke's decision to tell us something twice suggests that he wants us to learn from it (the issue is being generous, not necessarily selling all you own – we read later in Acts that believers still owned homes in which to meet).

2. Luke highlights Barnabas as an example to us. Luke tells us that Barnabas was originally called Joseph but the apostles had given him this special name, meaning 'Son of Encouragement'. The inclusion of this detail suggests that Luke is holding Barnabas up as a model for us.

3. Luke gives an opposite example to Barnabas. In Acts 5:1–11 we read about Ananias and Sapphira, who also sold some property and apparently gave all the proceeds to the apostles, while secretly they kept some money back for themselves. Peter condemns them, for, in claiming to be more generous than they were, they were guilty of lying to God. God then dramatically judges them. Luke tells us of this incident immediately after his mention of Barnabas, as though he is deliberately presenting both a positive and a negative example.

Given these points, there is good reason to take Barnabas as an example for us to follow. And given our materialistic culture, he is a very challenging one.

Worked example 2

Acts chapter 8 tells of how Philip takes the gospel to Samaria, and many believe. We then read this:

> When the apostles in Jerusalem heard that Samaria had accepted the word of God, they sent Peter and John to them. When they arrived, they prayed for them that they might receive the Holy Spirit, because the Holy Spirit had not yet come upon any of them; they had simply been baptised into the name of the Lord Jesus. Then Peter and John placed their hands on them, and they received the Holy Spirit.
>
> (Acts 8:14–17)

Some have concluded from this incident that, once people have become Christians, they need at some later date to receive the fullness of the Holy Spirit in an experience distinct from conversion. This is sometimes called 'baptism in the Spirit' or a 'second blessing'. However, when we look more closely we discover that is a case of mistakenly turning a description into a prescription. Note the following points:

1. This isn't what happens in the rest of the book of Acts: if every time someone became a Christian in Acts we saw this process repeated, it would be natural to conclude that Luke is presenting it as the normal Christian experience. However, that isn't the case. Elsewhere in the book, people receive the Spirit the moment they put their faith in Christ, just as Peter promises in Acts 2:38. (Acts 19 is not the exception that it might at first appear to be; those involved are most likely not true believers prior to their encounter with Paul.) Thus even within Acts, the experience of the Samaritans is highly unusual.

2. This is a unique moment in the history of the church. Acts 1:8 sets the agenda for all that will happen in the rest of the book; it is almost like a contents page:

> 'But you will receive power when the Holy Spirit comes
> on you; and you will be my witnesses in Jerusalem,
> and in all Judea and Samaria, and to the ends of the
> earth.'

As we read through Acts we see the Spirit-empowered preaching of Christ reach these three geographical regions / ethnic groups in turn – first the Jews in Jerusalem, then the Jews and Samaritans (kind of half-caste Jews) in Judea and Samaria, and then finally Gentiles from Rome, capital of the known world. Our verses from chapter 8 describe the very first time that the gospel has broken into Samaritan territory, stage 2 in the programme. This is an unrepeatable milestone in the spread of the gospel, the first time that the gospel has been preached to non-Jews. That's why the apostles, as founders of the church, come to investigate (again something that happens nowhere else in Acts). It is such a big development that the question is raised, 'Is this allowed? Can Samaritans really be Christians?' Of course, once they receive the Holy Spirit, everyone is convinced – this is proof that they are accepted by God. It seems that in this one-off case, God delayed in sending his Spirit until the right people were there to witness it. It would be a mistake to try to deduce what is normative from a unique occasion.

3. Other passages in the Bible forbid us from separating conversion from the Spirit's work. We must not draw principles from Acts 8 that lead us to contradict the plain teaching of other parts of Scripture. The following verses make clear that every converted person enjoys the Spirit's presence:

> If anyone does not have the Spirit of Christ, he does not belong
> to Christ.
> (Romans 8:9)

Having believed, you were marked in him with a seal, the
promised Holy Spirit.
(Ephesians 1:13)

In conclusion, there are several reasons why we should not take Luke's
description of the unique situation of the Samaritans as prescriptive for
the rest of the church today.

DIG DEEPER!

Read Genesis 37:1–11. Let's think about whether this
description of Joseph receiving dreams is an example
for us to follow or something unique to Joseph.
Ponder the following points:

Are there any indications in the passage that the
author wants us to see these dreams as an example,
or as something unique to Joseph?

If we read on in the story we find that Joseph's
dreams are fulfilled as he becomes second-in-com-
mand of Egypt, and so saves his family from
starvation (read Genesis 41 onwards). How does the
fact that Joseph plays such a key role in God's plan
affect your view of his dream as normal or unique?

What conclusions would you draw if you did take
this as an example? Do other parts of the Bible
confirm or deny those conclusions?

What conclusion have you come to? Is this an
example for us to follow or not?

15
The Bible Timeline Tool

The advice given by Leviticus 4:27–31 is pretty clear:

> If a member of the community sins unintentionally and does what is forbidden in any of the LORD's commands, he is guilty. When he is made aware of the sin he committed, he must bring as his offering for the sin he committed a female goat without defect. He is to lay his hand on the head of the sin offering and slaughter it at the place of the burnt offering. Then the priest is to take some of the blood with his finger and put it on the horns of the altar of burnt offering and pour out the rest of the blood at the base of the altar. He shall remove all the fat, just as the fat is removed from the fellowship offering, and the priest shall burn it on the altar as an aroma pleasing to the LORD. In this way the priest will make atonement for him, and he will be forgiven.

Now answer these questions honestly. Have you accidentally broken any of God's commandments this week? And have you slaughtered any female goats?

Well, why not? You believe in the Bible, don't you? So how come you're ignoring what it says?

The fact is, probably without even realizing it, you're using the Bible Timeline tool!

The Bible is a book with a big story, one that slowly unravels throughout human history. It begins at the start of Genesis with God creating the heavens and the earth (Genesis 1:1). It ends in the final chapters of the book of Revelation with God's people dwelling with him in a perfect new world, and God's enemies punished in hell. Lots happens in between! Perhaps the most important events are the Fall (where sin entered God's perfect world and everything went wrong) and the death and resurrection of Jesus (where things got put right). We can arrange those events on a simple Bible timeline (see figure 2).

Figure 2. A simple Bible timeline

To be honest, it's a pretty rubbish timeline, both for artistic reasons (those overlapping circles are supposed to be the stone rolled away from Jesus' tomb) and because we miss so much out. We'd really recommend you to get hold of 📖 *God's Big Picture* by Vaughan Roberts (IVP). It's a top book and will give you the Bible timeline in much more detail.

To use the Bible Timeline tool, we have to ask three simple questions:

1. Where is this passage on the Bible timeline?
2. Where am I on the Bible timeline?
3. How do I read this in the light of things that have happened in between?

Let's do that for the Leviticus passage above (see figure 3).

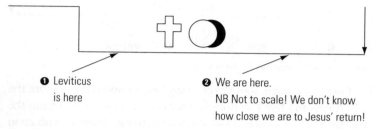

Figure 3. Bible timeline for Leviticus

How do we read Leviticus in the light of what has happened in between then and now, namely the death and resurrection of Jesus? His death was the final sacrifice for sins, the reality of which all the Old Testament sacrifices were just a 'shadow' (Hebrews 10:1). By the pouring out of Jesus' blood on the cross, we can be cleansed from all of our wrongs, both deliberate and accidental. For this reason, we don't have to kill goats any more.

That doesn't mean that Leviticus has got nothing to say to us. It teaches us that sin is very serious, that a death is needed to deal with it, that only by the shedding of blood can there be cleansing and forgiveness. We just have to read it through the lens of Christ's death to understand that those sacrifices have now been fulfilled. No wonder that Jesus said that throughout the Old Testament Scriptures there were things 'concerning himself' (Luke 24:27).

Another example comes from a recent Christian bestseller that has sparked huge controversy – we won't name it because that will just perpetuate its infamy. In one crucial passage, the author attacks traditional Christian teaching about original sin, complaining that 'Jesus believed in original goodness! God declared that all his creation, including humankind, was very good.'

Can you see where his use of Genesis 1:31 falls down in terms of the Bible timeline? (See figure 4.)

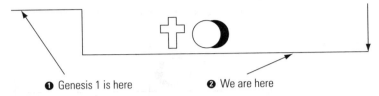

❶ Genesis 1 is here   **❷** We are here

Figure 4. Bible timeline for Genesis 1

God's statement about everything being good comes before the fall. Adam and Eve had not yet disobeyed God and eaten from the tree from which God had forbidden them to eat. There was no sin in the world. There was no death. Things certainly were 'very good'!

But that isn't the way the world is any more. In fact, only five chapters further on in Genesis we are told that 'the LORD saw how great man's wickedness on the earth had become, and that every inclination of the thoughts of his heart was only evil all the time' (Genesis 6:5).

There is now a huge problem of evil at the heart of our human nature. God cannot turn a blind eye to it. His holiness means he cannot coexist with sin; his justice means that he must punish it. Our only hope is Christ's death in our place, taking the punishment that we deserve.

All of these things are denied by the book in question. It twists what the Bible says, to create a message more agreeable to twenty-first-century ears. One of our prayers for this toolkit is that it will protect you against that kind of false teaching.

DIG DEEPER!

Read Genesis 13:14–17.

Some Christians take this to mean we should help modern-day Israel to evict the Palestinians from the Gaza Strip, since God has given the Israelites that land. What do you think of that idea?

Try using the Bible Timeline tool to answer our three questions:

1. Where is this passage on the Bible timeline?
2. Where am I on the Bible timeline?
3. How do I read this in the light of things that have happened in between? In particular, read Hebrews 11:16 to see what perspective that verse gives on the nature of the 'promised land'.

What is the true 'promised land' that Christians are looking forward to?

A timeline within a timeline

At the risk of making things too complicated, here is a modified 'Russian dolls' version of our timeline (see figure 5). It's supposed to indicate that the whole of the story is anticipated in miniature within the Old Testament.

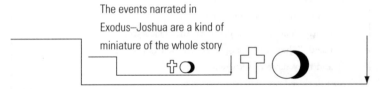

The events narrated in Exodus–Joshua are a kind of miniature of the whole story

Figure 5. A timeline within a timeline

Obviously Jesus doesn't die and rise again twice; that's not what we mean. But there are strong parallels between what happened to Moses and the Israelites in the fourteenth century BC and what has happened to us through Christ. They were slaves (in Egypt) but were redeemed (through the Passover) to be God's own people, awaiting the promised land (Canaan). We were slaves (to sin) but were redeemed (through the death and resurrection of Jesus) to be God's own people, awaiting the promised land (heaven).

This close correspondence between their situation and ours helps us in applying some parts of the Old Testament. Paul can even write the following to his New Testament audience:

For everything that was written in the past was written to
teach us, so that through endurance and the encouragement
of the Scriptures we might have hope.
(Romans 15:4)

These things happened to them as examples and were written
down as warnings for us, on whom the fulfilment of the ages
has come.
(1 Corinthians 10:11)

Worked example

Consider this warning from Psalm 95:

> Today, if you hear his voice,
>   do not harden your hearts as you did at Meribah,
>   as you did that day at Massah in the desert,
> where your fathers tested and tried me,
>   though they had seen what I did.
> For forty years I was angry with that generation;
>   I said, 'They are a people whose hearts go astray,
>   and they have not known my ways.'
> So I declared on oath in my anger,
>   'They shall never enter my rest.'
> (Psalm 95:7–11)

The psalm looks back to the events of Exodus 17, where the
Israelites, having just been miraculously rescued from Egypt, somehow
manage to doubt God's goodness to them. They're complaining
because they're in the desert and there's no water, and so they accuse
God of saving them only so that they will die of thirst. It's perverse
logic. Something very similar happens in the book of Numbers, and
ultimately it's because of this kind of rebellion that a whole generation
is excluded from entering the Promised Land. That is what is meant by
God's oath that 'they shall never enter my rest'.

The psalm urges its Old Testament readers not to be like that earlier generation, hardening their hearts to God's voice. However, it's also something picked up by the New Testament book of Hebrews:

> So, as the Holy Spirit says: 'Today, if you hear his voice, do not harden your hearts as you did in the rebellion, during the time of testing in the desert.'
> (Hebrews 3:7–8)

The writer to the Hebrews says the warning of Psalm 95, coming from that Exodus generation, now applies to Christians! This is a case of the miniature 'Russian dolls' timeline – their experience was a picture of ours. Just as they looked back to their salvation but forward to the promised land, so we can look back to the cross and forward to heaven. Just as they experienced a time of wandering in the desert before they received all that God had promised them, so we experience a time of waiting in this present world until we receive all that God has promised. In the midst of the wait, we need to make sure that we keep on trusting God's promises.

The writer to the Hebrews goes on:

> Therefore, since the promise of entering his rest still stands, let us be careful that none of you be found to have fallen short of it. For we also have had the gospel preached to us, just as they did; but the message they heard was of no value to them, because those who heard did not combine it with faith . . . Let us, therefore, make every effort to enter that rest, so that no-one will fall by following their example of disobedience.
> (Hebrews 4:1–2, 11)

We should learn from that previous generation the vital lesson of perseverance. We must keep trusting and obeying God's promise to us in Jesus right up until the day we enter God's rest.

As an aside, we don't think that this means that Christians can 'lose' their salvation. The rest of the Bible is pretty clear about that (e.g. Philippians 1:6; John 10:28–29). But that doesn't mean that we are free to ignore the warnings, either. It's a bit like having a 'DANGER, STEEP DROP' sign on the edge of a cliff. The presence of the sign doesn't mean that lots of people fall off; in fact, the sign is the means by which they don't. It would be stupid, though, to play around the edge.

When you don't need the Bible Timeline tool

There is one aspect to our Bible study that doesn't require the Bible Timeline tool, and that is when we look at the character of God. Our God is unchanging, forever the same:

I the LORD do not change.
(Malachi 3:6)

The Father of the heavenly lights . . . does not change like shifting shadows.
(James 1:17)

Jesus Christ is the same yesterday and today and for ever.
(Hebrews 13:8)

It doesn't matter whether you read about him in Deuteronomy or Habakkuk or Galatians or Revelation. In every one of those books, we're reading about the very same God that we pray to as our Father. That's why it's so wrong when people try to drive a wedge between the 'stern' God of the Old Testament and the 'kind' God of the New. (For one thing it means that they haven't read either Testament very carefully.) God is both stern *and* kind (Romans 11:22). He has not changed since the day that he rained down burning sulphur on Sodom and Gomorrah (Genesis 19:24). It's true that he now *delays* his judgment until the final day, but his anger at sin is no different. But neither has he changed from the tender shepherd that David knew him to be, who 'leads beside quite waters' and 'restores my soul' (Psalm 23).

DIG DEEPER!

Read Exodus 6:1–8.

What unchanging truths do you learn about God and his character?

What elements are there in the mini-story of Exodus that will parallel the big story?

16

The 'Who Am I?' Tool

It's true that the title of this tool implies existential angst. The point of it, though, is to work out which character (if any) we are supposed to identify with, in a given passage. If the Bible Timeline tool looked at the 'when' – 'When was this, relative to when I am?' – then this tool looks at the 'who' – 'Who is this, relative to who I am?'

I (Andrew) was once in a church home group studying Exodus chapter 3, which begins like this:

Now Moses was tending the flock of Jethro his father-in-law, the priest of Midian, and he led the flock to the far side of the desert and came to Horeb, the mountain of God. There the angel of the LORD appeared to him in flames of fire from within a bush. Moses saw that though the bush was on fire it did not burn up. So Moses thought, 'I will go over and see this strange sight – why the bush does not burn up.'
(Exodus 3:1–3)

We were working from published notes, and I still remember one of the questions: 'What burning-bush experiences have you had?'

It was a silly question. I was 99.9% sure that no-one in the group had ever seen a bush that was on fire but did not burn up, or heard the voice of God speaking from the middle of it. Not one of us had had a burning-bush experience.

Actually, that's not quite true. I once went to a firework party at the house of a friend in East London. Not being very experienced in setting up fireworks, someone had pushed the rocket so far into the launch tube that the end stuck out the other side into the ground beneath, anchoring it a little too firmly. When we lit the rocket, it started 'blasting off', but without going anywhere. It was one of those split-second things, as we all realized that it was about to detonate at ground level. 'Get back!' Followed by *boom!* as fire flew in all directions. Followed by *woof!* as the large fluffy pampas-grass bush in the next-door neighbour's garden was enveloped by a fireball. We reached for the garden hose, but it was all over for that bush within seconds. Almost a burning-bush experience. But, sadly for neighbourly relations, it was not miraculously kept from burning up.

Those Bible study notes fell foul of the Genre tool, effectively turning a historical narrative into a metaphor for our psychological experiences. But they also failed on account of the 'Who Am I?' tool. It was a story about Moses. And Moses isn't me.

The Moses-is-me syndrome (as we call it) reflects my propensity for identifying myself as the hero or central character in every story; everything has to be ultimately about me and my life. If someone shows you an old photograph of your class at school, who do your eyes go to first? Yourself. Well, so it is with the Bible. We read the story of Moses and the bush as though we were Moses. We read about David and Goliath as if we were David: what are the giants that you need to fight in your life? We read the story of Elisha doing mighty miracles through the Holy Spirit and we are Elisha. And so on.

But we shouldn't have to think very hard before we realize that none of us is the king who defeats God's enemies and rules over God's people (David), or the mediator who led his people out of slavery (Moses), or the one with power to heal lepers or raise the dead (Elisha). There is someone else who fits those descriptions much better than we do! Indeed, the ways in which the lives of these men prefigure the life of Christ is often remarkable. Think, for example, of how Pharaoh orders all Hebrew infants to be killed, but Moses manages to escape. Compare Herod's edict and Jesus' escape in Matthew 2. Or how about David's feeling of God-forsakenness as he pens Psalm 22? That psalm is so true to Jesus' experience that we easily forget that it was first used by someone else.

Having said all this, *sometimes* we are right to identify with Moses and David. For example, David's experience of God's forgiveness is something that we may share:

David . . . speaks of the blessedness of the man to whom God credits righteousness apart from works:

'Blessed are they
    whose transgressions are forgiven,
    whose sins are covered.
Blessed is the man
    whose sin the Lord will never count
      against him.'
(Romans 4:6–8, quoting Psalm 32)

Again, Moses' trust in God is something that the book of Hebrews encourages us to imitate:

By faith Moses, when he had grown up, refused to be known as the son of Pharaoh's daughter. He chose to be ill-treated along with the people of God rather than to enjoy the pleasures of sin for a short time. He regarded disgrace for the sake of Christ as of greater value than the treasures of Egypt, because he was looking ahead to his reward.
(Hebrews 11:24–26)

Mind you, sometimes the characters we should identify with aren't the heroes so much as the villains! For instance, we might be one of the grumbling Israelites whom Moses has to lead, rather than Moses himself (see 1 Corinthians 10:1–13). In David's lament psalms, we might sometimes be the persecutor rather than the victim. (That's how Paul applies some of these psalms to us in Romans 3:9–18.)

To sum up: often these Old Testament characters are pictures of Jesus and so we should learn from them about *him*, rather than about ourselves. However, sometimes these characters are role models (both positive and negative) for us. We just need to stop and think before we rush to put ourselves into the picture.

Worked example

What do you think the following verse means for us?

> But the Counsellor, the Holy Spirit, whom the Father will send in
> my name, will teach you all things and will remind you of
> everything I have said to you.
> (John 14:26)

If we assume that this was addressed directly to us, then we might conclude that we don't really need to read the Bible (and certainly don't need to bother with all these tools) because Jesus promised that the Holy Spirit would teach us everything directly.

However, Jesus wasn't addressing us in John 14. He was speaking to his apostles. What's more, he can't have been speaking to us, because he talks about reminding them of everything he said. We can't be reminded, because we didn't hear him say it in the first place.

The right question to ask, therefore, is: 'What does it mean to me that Jesus said this to them?' Answer: 'I can trust the New Testament. Jesus promised to those who wrote much of it that the Spirit would guide them into all truth, and give them perfect memories for his teaching.' This verse should make me want to read the Bible more, not less!

Having said that, there are other verses in the Bible that teach us about the Spirit's work in us and how he enables us to understand what God has given us (see 1 Corinthians 2:11–16). It's a wonderful thing to grasp that the Spirit both guarantees the Bible's trustworthiness and helps us to understand what was written.

DIG DEEPER!

Read Joshua 1:1–9.

The book of Joshua describes how Joshua leads Israel into the promised land, defeating their enemies. The Bible Timeline tool reminds us that this is a 'mini-picture' of God's rescue of us: through Jesus he defeats our enemy, the devil, and brings us to the promised land of heaven. Now let's use the 'Who Am I?' tool.

We might be tempted to put ourselves in Joshua's shoes, and so read God's words to him as if they applied directly to us. What do you think of that idea?

What is distinctive about Joshua's role in verse 6?

Instead of reading this verse as God speaking to all Christians, how could it be read as a picture of God commissioning Jesus as our leader?

So which group of people should we identify with in this passage?

17
The 'So What?' Tool

It is possible to be an expert in understanding the Bible and for it to do you no good whatsoever. You might apply the tools in this book with such care and precision that you know exactly what Paul meant when he wrote to the Romans, or what Isaiah was saying to the people in his day. That's interesting as a history lesson, but unless you recognize that God is also speaking through those things *to you today*, it will have been a waste of time. We must always ask the 'So what?' question. What does this mean for me and my life?

Actually, in the last three tools (Copycat, Bible Timeline, 'Who Am I?') we've been encouraging you not to jump *too quickly* to apply things to yourself. We need to take care to understand before we apply. But we must get to application in the end:

> Do not merely listen to the word, and so deceive yourselves.
> Do what it says. Anyone who listens to the word but does
> not do what it says is like a man who looks at his face in a
> mirror and, after looking at himself, goes away and
> immediately forgets what he looks like. But the man who
> looks intently into the perfect law that gives freedom, and

continues to do this, not forgetting what he has heard, but doing it – he will be blessed in what he does.
(James 1:22–25)

How then can we make sure that we 'do' the word? Stage 1 is to work out what response the author was looking for – the Author's Purpose all over again. Stage 2 is to work that out in the nitty-gritty of our lives. Here are two questions that might help:

- Do I need to stop doing something? Is there some aspect of my behaviour that must change?
- Is there something new that I should start doing?

However, it isn't only our actions that God wants to change. His word also addresses our patterns of thinking.

Motives matter

Over the years that I (Nigel) have been married, I have learnt that my wife really enjoys being bought flowers. But I'm not so bothered about that sort of thing myself, so I don't naturally think of bringing flowers home for her.

Imagine if I said to myself, 'It will make my life a lot easier if I get Elisa some flowers', and so I then buy her flowers mechanically once a month, looking for a quiet life. That isn't quite what Elisa had in mind! It's hardly romantic, is it?

However, imagine a second scenario. I say to myself, 'I know that Elisa really likes flowers, and I love her, so I'm going to get some flowers today.' Now we're all smiling!

The point is this: simply doing an action, in this case buying flowers, isn't enough. What lies behind the action is vitally important. The same is true for us as we apply the Bible to our lives.

Sometimes we are given direct commands:

Flee from sexual immorality.
(1 Corinthians 6:18)

> Bear with each other and forgive whatever grievances you
> may have against one another.
> (Colossians 3:13)

> 'A new command I give you: Love one another.'
> (John 13:34)

Obviously, the right response to these verses is to put them into
practice and obey what God says. However, our motives matter
too. We could do these things just to impress other Christians, or
because we think that going to heaven depends on our earning
our way through good works, or a host of other wrong reasons,
none of which would honour God.

Here is Paul's imperative from 1 Corinthians 6 in its context:

> Flee from sexual immorality. All other sins a man commits
> are outside his body, but he who sins sexually sins against his
> own body. Do you not know that your body is a temple of
> the Holy Spirit, who is in you, whom you have received from
> God? You are not your own; you were bought at a price.
> Therefore honour God with your body.
> (1 Corinthians 6:18–20)

Did you notice the motivations Paul gives for the command of
fleeing sexual immorality?

- We have the Holy Spirit living in us, so what we do with
  our bodies really matters.
- We have been bought by God. This picks up on the idea of
  redemption we encountered under the Vocabulary tool.
  God has paid the price of Jesus' death to buy us, so that we
  now belong to him.

Paul isn't moralizing. He doesn't just bark out a command and
expect us to follow it; he tells us *why* we should live differently. He

wants us to be gripped by the knowledge that we belong to God now, that his Spirit lives within us. As we grasp that as reality, we will be empowered to flee sexual immorality.

The Bible addresses not only our behaviour but our *worldview*, the mental map we have of the world. It should shape the way we see God, other people, ourselves.

Our worldview impacts how we live. If someone sees money as the most important thing in life, that person will pursue a career that pays as much as possible. If someone cares about the environment, that person will make time for recycling and composting. If someone believes that there is a loving God who made us and who sent his Son to die to save us, that person will live to please him. A biblical worldview leads to biblical behaviour.

In summary, we should ask of our Bible passage not only 'What does it tell me to do?' but also 'How does it tell me to think?'

Who is this message for?

Not every passage of the Bible will be equally relevant at every point in your life. Some passages are written to comfort the suffering, others to rebuke the complacent; they are for different times and seasons. We don't recommend being too selective in what you read, however; the ideal is to work through whole books bit by bit, and to cover the whole Bible in time. There are two reasons for this. First, you will store up lessons that you might need in the future when circumstances change. (The best time to get your thoughts clear on the issue of suffering is when you are *not* suffering.) Secondly, it will keep you from steering clear of the uncomfortable passages that, like bad-tasting medicine, may still be good for you.

That said, you will sometimes hear God saying something in the Scriptures that, while not immediately relevant to you, you realize would be a great help to *somebody else*. Sharing God's truth with one another within a Christian community is a wonderful thing. It's this that lies behind the vital spiritual gift of prophecy: 'Everyone who prophesies speaks to men for their strengthening, encouragement and comfort' (1 Corinthians 14:3).

At other times the Bible's message will apply not so much to 'me' or to 'you' but to 'us', corporately. Unlike modern English, the Bible's original languages have separate words for 'you' (singular) and 'you' (plural). It may be a challenge in our individualistic culture to realize that the plurals predominate. Take this example from Hebrews:

> See to it, brothers, that none of you has a sinful, unbelieving heart that turns away from the living God.
> (Hebrews 3:12)

That verse instructs the whole church ('brothers', plural) to ensure that no individual ('none of you', singular) falls away. Each person's spiritual well-being is the responsibility of everyone else.

Finally, it is good to ask what implications our passage has for someone who is not a believer. God has left us in the world to be his witnesses, and we are surrounded by those who do not know the saving power of the Lord Jesus – friends, family, colleagues, the cashier in the supermarket we shop in, the person we pass each day walking the dog. Our evangelism will be fired if we keep that person in mind as we read the Bible. We might read of a wonderful blessing that we have from God, and realize that they don't share it. Or we might read of the terrible danger from which we have been rescued, and realize that they have not been:

> The Father loves the Son and has placed everything in his hands. Whoever believes in the Son has eternal life, but whoever rejects the Son will not see life, for God's wrath remains on him.
> (John 3:35–36)

In summary, we should be asking what the passage means

- for you
- for a Christian friend

- for your church community
- for an unbeliever

Make sure you don't skip the 'you' part, though, lest you earn Jesus' rebuke: 'Why do you look at the speck of sawdust in your brother's eye and pay no attention to the plank in your own eye?' (Matthew 7:3).

Praying in response to what God has said

Sometimes people say that prayer is a two-way conversation, where God speaks to us and we speak to God. But the Bible never uses the word 'prayer' in this way. Prayer is simply when we talk to God.

Others think of reading the Bible as a conversation, in which God speaks to us, and we bring our own meanings to the text so that in some sense we find a voice too. That's not right, either.

We have a conversation when we hear God speak to us in the Bible and then we speak to him in prayer. There's a vivid description of that dynamic in Nehemiah chapters 8 – 9. For *seven days* Ezra the scribe read the words of the law of God (part of the Old Testament) to the people. As they heard God speaking to them, the people were deeply moved to sadness and to joy; there were tears as well as rejoicing and great feasting. And in response to what they heard, they poured out their hearts in prayer to God.

In our churches, though, the things that we share 'for prayer' at the end of an evening's Bible study are often completely unrelated to the passage we've been studying. While it's true that nothing is too small to bring before our heavenly Father, it's a shame when the tiny things – the health of someone's neighbour's dog – take over, and we forget the amazing truths that God has been speaking to us minutes before.

Get into the habit of praying these kinds of prayers:

- 'Sorry for X, which your word has shown to be wrong in my life.'

- 'Thank you for Y, which you have shown us this evening.'
- 'Please, by your Spirit, give me power to change Z in response to what you have been saying.'

Worked example

In Revelation 21 we read John's vision of God's new creation.

> Then I saw a new heaven and a new earth, for the first heaven and the first earth had passed away, and there was no longer any sea. I saw the Holy City, the new Jerusalem, coming down out of heaven from God, prepared as a bride beautifully dressed for her husband. And I heard a loud voice from the throne saying, 'Now the dwelling of God is with men, and he will live with them. They will be his people, and God himself will be with them and be their God. He will wipe every tear from their eyes. There will be no more death or mourning or crying or pain, for the old order of things has passed away.'
> (Revelation 21:1–4)

We aren't told specifically to do anything in this passage, but that doesn't mean it doesn't apply to us. It has much to say to how we view the world. It should make us ask questions like this:

- Do I really believe the world is heading to this wonderful future?
- Does this certain future give me a wonderful sense of hope and joy?
- Am I looking forward to this day?

All of those questions are to do with our worldview. As we change the way we think, it will surely lead to changes in how we live.

If we had spent some time looking at the Author's Purpose, we would have discovered that the book of Revelation is addressed to suffering Christians (see 1:9). So we might also ask of our passage:

- How does this future change the way I view suffering in the present?

- Is there someone in my church who is undergoing suffering, whom I could encourage with these verses?

We might also ask ourselves what this passage means for friends who are not believers. This is a glorious vision of a future that they will miss out on, unless they trust in Christ. Should we not tell them of it?

Finally, what sort of prayers should we be praying in response to this passage?

- 'Thank you, Father, that you have prepared this amazing future for your people.'
- 'Please help me to live to today in the light of this promise. I pray that you would give me a heavenly perspective on that essay deadline / problem at work / trouble with the kids that has dominated my horizons recently.'
- 'I pray for my Christian friend who is dying of cancer. Please comfort her in the hope that one day there will be no more death or mourning or crying or pain.'
- 'Lord, have mercy on the person who I see at the bus stop every day. Give me an opportunity to speak to him about Jesus, so that he too might have a place in your new heaven and new earth.'

DIG DEEPER!

We quoted Colossians 3:13 above but left out part of the verse. Read this verse in the context of verses 1–14.

What motivations are given to forgive?

Think about what the Lord has done for you. How does that change your worldview (values, priorities, view of yourself and of others)?

How will this help you forgive other Christians? Try to be very practical.

What would be an appropriate prayer in light of what you have learned?

Pray that prayer!

Conclusion:
Pulling It All Together

Imagine watching a carpenter at work. Holes have been drilled, angles cut, joints made, and now the scene is chaotic with tools and bits of wood everywhere. But then comes the moment when all the parts are assembled and at last you can see what all the activity has been about. Aha! It's a chair!

The same moment comes when we are studying the Bible. The tools we've mentioned can all play a part in helping you understand different aspects of your Bible passage, but the time comes to draw together all you have learnt.

It is a very good discipline to try to capture the overall message of your passage in a single sentence or soundbite. Writing a sentence sounds quite an easy thing to do, but actually it's one of the hardest. You will have discovered many things, but we're asking you to boil it down to just one or two big ideas. You need to decide what is central and what is peripheral; which of your insights should go in the margin, and which should be written in block capitals with a box around them. What lies at the heart of all that God has been saying to you?

Imagine you finish your Bible study and get on a bus to go into town. There's a spare seat next to someone you know, and you get chatting.

'What have you been doing this afternoon?' your friend asks.

'I've been reading the Bible.'

'Oh yes? What did you find out?'

'Well . . .'

Cue your summary sentence. In a few words you are able to answer your friend's question. The essence of the passage is at your fingertips; it's concrete in your mind and you're taking it with you wherever you go.

Here are a few hints on writing a summary sentence.

- Don't make it too long. It's tempting to try and cram in everything you've learnt, but that defeats the object. You're aiming to focus on the main point.
- Try to distinguish between the overall point of a passage and the subsidiary or supporting points.
- Make sure your sentence has sense of purpose in it. We don't want just to learn abstract, academic truths. God never speaks to us simply to give us information; he always speaks with a purpose, and it will be helpful to reflect that in your sentence.
- Use your sentence to meditate on what God has said to you through the day.

Worked example

Sing joyfully to the LORD, you righteous;
    it is fitting for the upright to praise him.
Praise the LORD with the harp;
    make music to him on the ten-stringed lyre.
Sing to him a new song;
    play skilfully, and shout for joy.

For the word of the LORD is right and true;
he is faithful in all he does.
The LORD loves righteousness and justice;
the earth is full of his unfailing love.

By the word of the LORD were the heavens made,
their starry host by the breath of his mouth.
He gathers the waters of the sea into jars;
he puts the deep into storehouses.
Let all the earth fear the LORD;
let all the people of the world revere him.
For he spoke, and it came to be;
he commanded, and it stood firm.
(Psalm 33:1–9)

We put the toolkit to work on the passage above. Here are some of the things we came up with.

Using the Structure tool, we have split the psalm in half at verse 9. For the sake of space, we will look at only the first half.

The Tone and Feel tool should get you reaching for a tambourine! This is a celebration song, full of praise to God (verses 1–3).

The Genre tool tells you that this is poetry. There aren't literal 'storehouses' (verse 7) in which God puts the waters of the deep. It's a way of telling you that he is in control of all of nature – he decides when it rains and when there is a drought, almost as if he stores the water away for the time that he sees fit.

Let's move on to the Quotation/Allusion tool. The reference to God creating the world by a word (verse 6) looks back to Genesis 1:3, in which God merely says, 'Let there be light', and there is light. That tells you something about the authority of God's words, doesn't it? If I were to say, 'Launch missiles against China now', nothing would happen (except my getting a reputation for extreme political views). If the President of the United States of America says, 'Launch missiles against

China now', then there will be a third world war. But even the
American President can go into the Oval Office and say, 'Let there be
light' as much as he likes, and unless he's gone to ridiculous lengths
with electronics and voice-recognition software, it won't do much.
God's words have unsurpassed power.

What about the Translations tool? Instead of the reference to the
waters being put into jars (verse 7), some more literal versions have
this curious expression: 'He gathers the waters of the sea together as
a heap' (Psalm 33:7, NASB). It's not surprising that the NIV opted for a
different rendering, because water doesn't really form 'heaps'; it tends
to flow away! Nonetheless, the word 'heap' is in the original Hebrew.
Maybe we can see why, if we bring in the Quotations/Allusions tool
again. There are two references to heaps of water in the Old
Testament, both of them in the context of God providing safe passage
for his people on their journey out of slavery in Egypt and into the
promised land:

> At the blast of Your nostrils the waters were piled up,
> The flowing waters stood up like a heap.
> (Exodus 15:8, NASB)

> Now the Jordan is in flood all during harvest. Yet as soon as the
> priests who carried the ark reached the Jordan and their feet touched
> the water's edge, the water from upstream stopped flowing. It piled
> up in a heap a great distance away . . . So the people crossed over
> opposite Jericho.
> (Joshua 3:15–16)

Please don't worry if you wouldn't have got that for yourself. We
only found these references because we've got a computer program
that allowed us to do a search on the Hebrew word for 'heap'.
Cheating! This insight is a bonus, but certainly not something essential
for understanding the passage.

The Parallels tool really comes into its own in the Psalms. There are parallels everywhere! We'll look at three that help our understanding in some way:

> For the word of the LORD is right and true
>   he is faithful in all he does.
> (Psalm 33:4)

You might expect the second line to say that God is faithful in all he *says*. But instead, the author parallels a statement about God's word with a statement about his action. That is because God acts by speaking, as we've noted already.

> By the word of the LORD were the heavens made
>   their starry host by the breath of his mouth.
> (verse 6)

Here the 'word' of God is paralleled with the 'breath of his mouth'. Fair enough, because words travel on our breath, as we mentioned near the start of this book. However, we can go further. In Hebrew, the word for 'breath' is the same as the word for 'Spirit'. The parallel is telling us that what God accomplishes through his Spirit is the same as what he accomplishes by his word.

There's one more case where the Parallels tool will help us, and in fact it comes to the aid of the Vocabulary tool. You might have wondered what it means to 'fear the LORD' in verse 9. Does it mean a spooky, horror-movie kind of fear? Or an anxious 'What will happen?' fear? Or a terrified, waiting-outside-the-head-teacher's-office fear? No, none of these:

> Let all the earth fear the LORD;
>   let all the people of the world revere him.
> (verse 8)

'Fear' is paralleled with reverence. To fear God is to hold him in awe, to respect him.

What about the Repetition tool? Notice that God's word or the fact that he speaks is mentioned in three separate verses (verses 4, 6, 8). Similarly, his work of creation features a fair bit. These are two themes to which we must give due weight.

Next up is the Linking Words tool. Twice we get a 'for' that links the imperative to praise/fear God with a reason for doing so, namely that God made everything by speaking. Here is the second one:

> Let all the earth fear the LORD;
>   let all the people of the world revere him.
> $\overleftarrow{For}$ he spoke, and it came to be;
>   he commanded, and it stood firm.
> (verses 8–9)

Noticing this logical relationship actually helps us to unlock the Structure of the whole section:

Verses 1–3	Instruction to praise God
Verses 4–7	*Reason*: he is the Creator
Verse 8	Instruction to revere God
Verse 9	*Reason*: he is the Creator

Do we need to be worried by the Bible Timeline tool? Not really. We are being told something timeless about God, who never changes.

Similarly, the 'Who Am I?' tool will not cause us much difficulty. The audience envisaged in verse 8 is 'all the people of the world', and we can fairly confidently place ourselves in that category!

All the work of the 'So What?' tool has been done for us by the author in this case. He tells us exactly what response he is looking for – we are to praise God (verses 1–3) and revere him (verse 8). And so is every human being who lives on this planet.

Phew! All those tools later, how are you feeling? Exhausted? Confused? Learnt lots but unsure how it all fits together?

This is the stage when we need to be ruthless. Which of our insights were central, and which can we leave to one side? The 'waters in a heap' thing – that can go. The centrality of God's word in creation – that must stay, because it was supported by converging evidence from more than one tool.

Some agonizing decisions later, here is our attempt at a summary sentence:

God created the cosmos by his word, so fear him.

Maybe you can do better, but hopefully you agree that we're in the right ball park.

The Andromeda galaxy is the closest to our own, only 2.2 million light years away. It's so wide that if you started at one end and flew to the other on Concorde, it would take you 125 billion years (my rough calculation). It contains something like 10,000 million stars, each one of them like our own sun. The LORD made it all. By just telling it to exist. Wow!

Respect is due to a God like that. That is what Psalm 33:1–9 is telling us.

DIG DEEPER!

This is the last chapter in the book, and we don't have another exercise. Well, actually, we do. Pick a book of the Bible. Any book. Start using the tool-kit. Listen to what God is saying. Have your life changed. Then move on to the next book and do the same.

We can think of no better closing remarks than those of Paul to the elders of the church in Ephesus:

'Now I commit you to God and to the word of
his grace, which can build you up and give you
an inheritance among all those who are
sanctified.'
(Acts 20:32)

Recommended Reading

Maybe this doesn't need saying, but the book that we'd most recommend that you read after this one is ... the Bible. Seriously. But we thought we'd suggest some other things for you to read as well. Those marked * are more difficult or academic, which doesn't necessarily make them better.

Maybe you have been conscious while reading this book that you're not a Christian, or not a *real* one at least – you don't know Christ as your own Lord and Saviour. Although we've tried to touch on some of the core truths of the Christian gospel in passing, there are other books that set it out more simply and clearly. We recommend

- 📖 *Christianity Explored* by Rico Tice and Barry Cooper (Carlisle: Authentic Lifestyle, 2002)
- 📖 *Turning-Points* by Vaughan Roberts (Carlisle: Authentic Lifestyle, 2002)
- 📖 *A Fresh Start* by John Chapman (Sydney: Matthias Media, 2003)

There are some other books which cover similar ground to this one. If we've failed and you want to check out another approach (or you just want more of the same), then you could try

- 📖 *Postcard from Palestine* by Andrew Reid (Sydney: Matthias Media, 1997)
- 📖 *Grasping God's Word: A Hands-on Approach to Reading, Interpreting and Applying the Bible* by J. Scott Duvall and J. Daniel Hays (Grand Rapids: Zondervan, 2001)
- 📖 *How to Read the Bible for All Its Worth* by Gordon Fee and Douglas Stuart (Grand Rapids: Zondervan, 2003)

If you want to turn your understanding of a Bible passage into some study questions to help others understand the passage for themselves either in a small group or a one-to-one setting, try

- *Growth Groups* by Colin Marshall (Sydney: Matthias Media, 1995)
- *One to One: A Discipleship Handbook* by Sophie DeWitt (Carlisle: Authentic Lifestyle, 2003)

For a fuller critique of postmodernism, the mindset that says that there is no absolute meaning in a text, only what it means 'to me' (a notion that we attacked in chapter 1), see

- *Meltdown* by Marcus Honeysett (Leicester: IVP, 2002)
- **The Gagging of God* by Don Carson (Grand Rapids: Zondervan, 1995)

For a more detailed explanation of the 'inspiration' and 'authority' of the Bible (chapter 2) see

- *Bible Doctrine* by Wayne Grudem (Leicester: IVP, 1999).

The Bible Timeline tool gave a very rough sketch of the big story of the Bible and how it all fits together. We'd urge you to read something further on this:

- *God's Big Picture* by Vaughan Roberts (Leicester: IVP, 2003)
- **According to Plan: The Unfolding Revelation of God in the Bible* by Graeme Goldsworthy (Leicester: IVP, 2002)

Under the Vocabulary tool we recommended that you buy a Bible dictionary for reference. The best one to go for is probably

- *New Bible Dictionary* edited by Howard Marshall et al. (Leicester: IVP, 1996)

Finally, there are Bible commentaries. If you use them as a shortcut to the 'right answer' without doing the work on the text for yourself, they will make all that you have learnt in this book a waste of time. Be disciplined. Study a passage by yourself first for an hour or so, and only then turn to a commentary for further insight or help with a problem that you've run into. And remember, the commentary won't necessarily be right all the time!

We're not going to attempt to tell you the 'best' commentary on every Bible book: we don't have the expertise for that, for one thing. Instead, we thought we'd give you an assortment of commentaries that we've found particularly helpful. Some of them are part of a good series (in brackets after the title):

- *Genesis* by Bruce Waltke with Cathi Fredricks (Grand Rapids: Zondervan, 2001)
- 2 *Samuel* (Focus on the Bible) by Dale Ralph Davis (Fearn: Christian Focus, 1999)
- *Psalms* (Tyndale Old Testament Commentary) by Derek Kidner (Leicester: IVP, 1973), 2 volumes
- *The Message of Zechariah* (The Bible Speaks Today) by Barry Webb (Leicester: IVP, 2003)
- *The Gospel According to John* (Pillar Commentary) by D. A. Carson (Leicester: Apollos, 1991)
- *Romans* (New International Commentary on the New Testament) by Douglas Moo (Grand Rapids: Eerdmans, 1996)
- *The Message of 2 Timothy* (The Bible Speaks Today) by John Stott (Leicester: IVP, 1973)
- 1 *Peter* (Tyndale New Testament Commentary) by Wayne Grudem (Leicester: IVP, 1988)
- *Revelation Unwrapped* by John Richardson (Baulkham Hills: MPA Books, 1996)

Appendix: It Really Works!

Ed Shaw leads the work among university students at Christ Church, Clifton, in Bristol. They've been using the toolkit idea in their small groups. We asked Ed to explain what they did:

'As we seek to prepare the students that come to our church for a lifetime of Christian service, we're keen both to teach them God's word and for them to learn how to understand and apply it for themselves. With these aims in mind we found the toolkit provided in this book invaluable.

'At the beginning of the student year we trained up our small-group leaders to use the toolkit, with worked examples all taken from John's Gospel (the book that we were about to study). The aim was for them to teach the various tools to the students in their groups as appropriate passages came up over the course of the term. Each of our small groups had a set of large laminated cardboard cut-out tools (hammer, screwdriver, etc.) as a visual aid, each one corresponding to one of the tools from this book. One group produced a makeup bag equivalent! We also gave each student a small Bible-sized card with the whole toolkit on it and a brief explanation of each tool.

'Leaders chose to use the tools in different ways. Some explained a relevant tool at the beginning of the study, telling group members to be on the alert, looking for how it could be used during the evening. Others introduced the tool during the study as and when they reached a verse or paragraph where the tool would be helpful. Some small groups occasionally split into pairs, each armed with a different tool, to see which would help us most in understanding the passage. As the term progressed, all the tools were put on display from the beginning and group members had to work out which would be best to unlock the passage we were studying; we wanted to get them to a position where they were confident in using them for themselves.

'This visual way of teaching Bible-study skills proved memorable and effective. It's been a great encouragement to see students using the toolkit in Bible studies ever since. The result has been students handling God's word with increasing confidence and faithfulness; some have discovered important truths for the first time, and lives have been changed.

'We're keen to keep using the toolkit with each lot of new students who join the group. Competence in handling the Bible is one of the greatest needs in the church today and so this toolkit couldn't be more timely. I'd strongly urge you to get on and use it yourself and then teach it to others – the long-term benefit of doing that here in the UK and abroad is incalculable.'